Scully

STUDIO SCRIPTS
Series editor: David Self

Working
The Boy with the Transistor Radio *Willy Russell*
Good Prospects *Charlie Stafford*
Strike *Yolanda Casey*
George and Mildred *Johnnie Mortimer and Brian Cooke*
Emmerdale Farm *Douglas Watkinson*

City Life
Lies I, II *Willy Russell*
Uncle Sangi *Tom Hadaway*
Short Back and Sides, I, II *Alan Plater*

Love and Marriage
Gulpin *Sheila Fay and Ken Jones*
First Date *David Williams*
The Fight *David Williams*
Just Love *Leonard Kingston*
I Cried at your Wedding *Madeline Sotheby*
Mum, Where are You? *Eric Paice*

Situation Comedy
Rising Damp *Eric Chappell*
Last of the Summer Wine *Roy Clarke*
Going Straight *Dick Clement and Ian la Frenais*
Happy Ever After *John Chapman and Eric Merriman*
The Liver Birds *Carla Lane*

School
Grange Hill *Phil Redmond*
The Little Dissident *George Baker*
Maids the Mad Shooter *Farrukh Dhondy*
Headmaster *John Challen*
Name in the Papers *David Williams*

Situation Comedy 2
Open All Hours *Roy Clarke*
Only When I Laugh *Eric Chappell*
Hancock's Half Hour *Roy Galton and Alan Simpson*
A Fine Romance *Bob Larbey*
Yes Minister *Antony Jay and Jonathan Lynn*

Boys from the Blackstuff *Alan Bleasdale*

Blood Brothers *Willy Russell*

Sport

Radio Scripts

Scully

Alan Bleasdale
Edited by David Self

STUDIO SCRIPTS

Hutchinson
London Melbourne Sydney Auckland Johannesburg

Hutchinson Education

An imprint of Century Hutchinson Ltd
62-65 Chandos Place, London WC2N 4NW

Century Hutchinson Australia Pty Ltd
PO Box 496, 16-22 Church Street, Hawthorn,
Victoria 3122, Australia

Century Hutchinson New Zealand Limited
PO Box 40-086, Glenfield, Auckland 10, New Zealand

Century Hutchinson South Africa (Pty) Limited
PO Box 337, Bergvlei 2012, South Africa

First published 1984
Reprinted 1987

Set in Century Schoolbook

Printed and bound in Great Britain by
Anchor Brendon Ltd, Tiptree, Essex

British Library Cataloguing in Publication Data

Bleasdale, Alan
  Scully — (Studio scripts)
  I. Title   II. Self, David   III. Series
  822'.914   PR6052.L397

ISBN 0 09 159481 2

Contents

Alan Bleasdale on Scully

Scully isn't about football; it isn't about Liverpool F.C. and a young fan's worship of that great player, Kenny Dalglish. It could happen anywhere in the world. I really do believe that. I may be completely wrong but, for me, *Scully* is all about dreams and the danger that they can turn into nightmares. Watch out.

We all have dreams. Try to keep them for as long as you can, and finally, if you can, do something about them. As Kenny Dalglish (football's answer to Robert Redford?) says in the series, 'Dreams alone are not enough.' I had dreams. Mine, indeed, were to play football for Liverpool and England, meet Sophia Loren and make her melt into my arms, retire at the age of twenty-five, buy my mum and dad the biggest mansion on Merseyside, and then sit in the sun for the next forty years – with Sophia Loren at my side. None of these dreams ever happened. Instead, in desperation, I became a playwright. And now I spend my days writing dreams. And nightmares. I hope you enjoy those dreams and nightmares that follow. . . .

Alan Bleasdale
June 1984

Introduction

Granada Television filmed some of the football sequences for its production of these *Scully* television plays before a Liverpool–Everton 'derby' at Anfield. Immediately the supporters on the famous Kop roared their approval, chanting, 'There's only one Franny Scully!'

Franny (or Francis) Scully has long been a Merseyside hero. He first came to life around 1968 when his creator, Alan Bleasdale, was a teacher, working in a boys' school in Huyton, which is a part of Liverpool. 'They were big, beefy fifteen-year-old lads built like three dockers welded together, and they had been given *Janet and John* books to read. I decided to write a story for them set in their own parish.'

So began the Scully stories. They were later broadcast on BBC Radio Merseyside and Radio 4. Bleasdale also wrote a full-length television *Play for Today* called *Scully's New Year's Eve*. Between 1975 and 1979, *The Franny Scully Show* was broadcast regularly on Liverpool's commercial radio station, Radio City, and the stories were published in the *Liverpool Daily Post*. There have also been two novels, *Scully* and *Who's Been Sleeping in My Bed?*, the latter being republished as *Scully and Mooey*, to coincide with the television adaptation of the stories. The seven-part television series was made in 1984 by Granada Television and first shown in that year on Channel 4. It was made entirely on location (and on film) and followed the success of the author's

Boys from the Blackstuff television drama series (the scripts of which are also available in *Studio Scripts*).

The Characters

In all the versions of the stories, **Scully** is almost sixteen and in his last year at school. He goes to a Catholic comprehensive school and is very good at drama which he loathes: 'Do I look as though I wear a bra?' he asks. He has a very different ambition which is to play professional football and he lives in hope that his favourite teacher, Mr Stevens (or **Steve**) will get him a trial. Before becoming a science teacher, Steve was a player with Blackburn Rovers.

In the television serial, one result of Scully's passion for football is that people he is talking to keep turning into his hero, the Liverpool and Scotland player, **Kenny Dalglish**. These are not ordinary daydreams. As Scully says, 'What's really worrying me is that I haven't got any control over seeing Kenny Dalglish. He keeps bein' there.' Although this is often very funny to the viewer and reader, Bleasdale has made the point that, '*Scully* is about what happens when a boy's dreams turn into nightmares. It is a morality tale.'

Scully's home life is nearly as strange. His father no longer lives at home:

He couldn't keep off the ale. All morning he'd sit there on the couch and promise her he wouldn't have another drink, and then all afternoon he'd make a liar out of himself. He was a good skin, me dad, when he was sober, but he wasn't sober much, and he was always out of work. So, one Saturday night last year me Mam bolted all the doors and wouldn't let him in when he fell down the path at a quarter to twelve. He sat on the porch for a bit and cried and then he went off. Next we heard, he'd bunked in with Dorothy, the crosseyed barmaid out of the Black Horse. She's so crosseyed she must have a magnet up her nose.

The Scully home is ruled by **Mrs Scully**, alternately

dominating and long-suffering. In the television scripts we also meet Scully's habitually hung-over **Gran** and two of his elder brothers: **Henry**, who thinks only of railways and spends his time listening to recordings of train noises; and work-shy **Tony**. Tony's girlfriend is called **Rita** but, as the series develops, we see that Tony is more interested in a neighbour, **Mrs Florrie Barrett** (who is his mother's age). Also in the household is Scully's younger brother, **Arthur**, who is aged nine and happily into transvestism.

Scully's best mate is **Mooey** who used to go to Scully's school but who now goes to a special school. As Scully puts it, 'He was dead chuffed when he got there. It was like winning the scholarship for him. He'd been trying for ages but he kept passing the tests they set him.' Ever cheerful, his catch phrase is the distinctive Merseyside word of approval, 'Yis!' (or, when very pleased, 'Double yis!').

Scully also spends a lot of time with **Mad Dog**, who is in his class at school.

Mad Dog's called Mad Dog because he is one. He's crackers, I'm not kidding. If he bites anyone they get rabies. Guaranteed. And **Snotty Dog's** got a running nose. It runs so fast it enters races. As for poor old Half A Dog, he's only got half a nose. Right from the start, when he was born, like, he's never had any bone there in the middle. They haven't given up tho' at the Hospital. They keep trying to give him one. He's had hundreds of operations. His Mum's written off for a nose transplant for him for Christmas. The Dogs' real name is O'Gorman but after their Dennis went to our school years ago and his initials were DOG, the whole family got nicknamed 'the Dogs' an' everyone calls their house 'the Dogs' Home'.

(Half A Dog does not appear in the television scripts, but we often hear the baby brother, **Puppy Dog.**)

Also in Scully's class are **Joey Kelly**, 'the classic school bully – a thug who is brave only when he has fifteen men standing behind him', and **Brian Bignall** – famous for his prowess as a fighter but not a bully.

Among the other recurring characters are:

Mrs Heath, Scully's distinctly middle-class English teacher and producer of the school pantomime;

'Dracula', the fiendish school caretaker: wide-eyed and fang-toothed, he develops a fondness for Mrs Scully;

'Castanets', his assistant, so-called because of his ill-fitting false teeth; given to repeating the last word of each of Dracula's sentences;

'Isaiah', a far from friendly local policeman;

Marie Morgan, Mooey's elder sister, fond of wearing black leather and not particularly modest with it; and

Joanna, a black girl, at first noticed only casually by Scully but with whom he obviously has a mutual, caring interest.

Liverpool

Part of the success of *Scully* is due to the fact that it is rooted so firmly in its Merseyside setting.

For many years, Liverpool was the second most important seaport in Britain and also a major industrial centre. Flour milling, sugar refining, electrical engineering and the manufacture of soap, margarine and chemicals have been among its major industries; and with its eleven kilometres of docks, it has been an important exporting and importing centre.

In the public mind, it has also achieved fame as the home of a brilliant football club and of another very good one. It is also the birthplace of many famous comedians and, of course, of the Beatles. Its inhabitants are famous for their wit and humour and for their spirit.

However, in recent years, Liverpool has suffered badly from the recession and the decline in traditional industries and trade. Unimaginative clearance of inner city areas has resulted in acres of waste land and up-rooted people living in tower blocks in places such as Kirkby. Urban decay, vandalism and unemployment have become the main features of the 'media' image of a once-thriving port. A recent magazine article summarized the problem and one effect of the government's response following the 1981 Toxteth Riots:

Several times in recent years the city of Liverpool has been the centre of national interest. First there were the Toxteth riots, and more recently the threatened bankruptcy of the city by the Labour council in rejection of government proposals on local spending.

Two elements have generated these sparks: the gradual economic desolation of the city itself, particularly since the war, and the biting self-respect of the people, who refuse to be set aside. Physically, Liverpool has been an increasingly depressing city to visit or live in. Part of Michael Heseltine's approach as Minister for Merseyside was to have trees planted to beautify the environment. A lot of them were stolen.

Arts Express, May 1984

Scully's response is direct. (See page 49.) How the quality of his future might have been better if the trees had had a chance to grow is a matter for debate.

Dialect
Liverpool is also the home of the distinctive Merseyside or Scouse dialect. (Scouse, or rather Lobscouse, was originally a food rather than the dialect. Made from cheap cuts of meat, potatoes and onions, it was, and still is, a kind of stew.)

The dialect delights in diminutives (Franny for Francis, Lanny for Landing Stage, corpy for corporation, etc.) and in dropped final consonants (la for lad, etc.)

Bleasdale's excellent ear for dialogue means that the speeches in *Scully* come easily off the page, but the occasional phrase may cause a momentary problem for the uninitiated. Two phrases in particular recur: 'Come 'head' (= come ahead, come on) and 'it's last' (= it's worst, terrible, etc.) To wag off is to play truant.

Interestingly, the television production of *Scully* was made by Granada Television's features department, almost as if it could not be decided whether it was a 'real' drama serial, a situation comedy or a documentary. Certainly it is highly realistic. Even the fantasy sequences have a strange kind of mad logic to them.

Some would say it is tragically realistic. Many scenes, particularly in the final episodes, are very moving. At the same time, *Scully* is a very funny picture of teenage life in an inner city environment and to find so many laughs in such a situation is a measure of Alan Bleasdale's achievement.

Using the Scripts

The most informal classroom reading of a playscript is helped by rehearsal. Even a very experienced professional actor prefers to look over his part before a first reading in front of his colleagues. In the classroom therefore, those who will be reading should be given time to look over their lines: to make sure that they know when to pause, when to 'interrupt' the previous speech, and to work out the changing mood of their character before they are asked to read aloud.

It is much easier to read to a group from the front of a traditional classroom, and from a standing position or a position where you can be seen by your audience. It may be helpful to appoint a 'director' who will decide the location of various settings and rehearse the actors in basic movements, checking that they know when and where to enter and exit.

Note that it is possible for a group to break into smaller groups, and for each of these to rehearse its own interpretation of one or more scenes, and then present their versions in turn to the whole class.

Even if you have seen the television production of *Scully*, resist the temptation to copy the screen version. Study the scripts and work out your own interpretations.

The scripts are presented as they were written by Alan Bleasdale. Some minor cuts were made in production simply because of the demands of timing: each episode fits a

25-minute 'slot'. (The final, rather more dramatic episode which brings together many of the story-lines is of fifty minutes' duration.) Some slight modifications have been made to the scripts for school use and some directions have been adapted so that they can be read easily in the classroom or drama studio by a 'narrator'.

Note that, provided these directions are read sympathetically, a television script will read just as fluently in the classroom as will any other kind of play; but it should not be forgotten that (like any good television play) it was conceived in visual terms. It will therefore be fruitful to discuss (as the original director must have done) where and how each scene should be 'shot' to realize the author's intentions.

Television plays on stage

A distinguishing feature of television plays is that, unlike stage plays, they can make speedy transitions from one scene to another. They can also include location scenes such as Anfield Football Ground, the M6 motorway or Otterspool Promenade.

The scripts in this volume will work successfully on stage, however, if they are given a stylized production either in the round or on a proscenium stage. Specially taken 35 millimetre slides, projected scenery or captions can announce locations to an audience, and the use of sound effects can be an effective substitute for detailed scenery (especially in, for example, school or street scenes). Exterior scenes (such as the football scenes in episode one) could be created by the use of slides, taped voices and sound effects. The use of stage furniture should be restricted so as to preserve fluency and speed of staging and one composite stage set could be designed to represent Scully's home.

Fantasy sequences might be re-created either by bathing the acting area in an 'unreal' colour (e.g. red for the Dracula scenes), the use of music (e.g. to suggest the ride of the 'cavalry' at the end of episode one) or perhaps by focusing a sharp-edged spotlight on the character involved (e.g. on 'Dalglish').

Part of the success of any television play lies in the fact that it can cut from one scene to another; and, in a stage performance of a television play, lighting changes must be used to effect such 'jump-cuts' from one part of the acting area to another.

Note that several episodes of *Scully* could be adapted to form a full-length play, and such an exercise in adaptation could involve useful language work or a project in a drama course. Permission for any performance must however be sought in advance (see page 4).

Scully (Andrew Schofield) listens to advice he does not like from 'Steve' (David Ross)

Episode 1

Scully
Mooey
Mad Dog
Snotty Dog
Kenny Dalglish, the Liverpool footballer
Mr Flanagan, Scully's probation officer
Steve (Mr Stevens), a teacher
Mrs Heath, another teacher
Dracula (Mr Moss), the school caretaker
Castanets (Mr Banks), his assistant
Joey Kelly
Brian Bignall (non-speaking part)
Red-haired boy (younger than Scully and his friends)
Joanna, a black girl

Episode 1

---

1   A training ground

We see **Scully** *training with Liverpool F.C.*

2   Liverpool F.C. Dressing Room

Scully *is changing with the Liverpool players.*

3   The players' tunnel

Scully *is running up the players' tunnel to the roars of the crowd,* **Dalglish's** *number seven shirt on his back.*

4   The school bike shed

After the last three scenes, we now see the reality: the back of a tired comprehensive school on a housing estate. We focus on the bike sheds. There are a few bikes, and some shadows in the corner. We close in and see **Scully** *in those shadows. He is sitting cross-legged and concentrating, paint brush in hand, as if trying to get some perspective on the subject. We see a tight little smile of satisfaction, before he glances sly-eyed at the camera. We still do not see his achievement.*

He stands and peeps out into the daylight: there is nobody there. He takes a pace or two out of the bike sheds, brush and paint box in his hand.

*As he does so, we see the **red-haired boy,** a much smaller lad who is in Second Year Seniors. He walks around the corner of the bike sheds, carrying a school register. **Scully** darts back into the shadows as the **boy** appears, but the **boy** has seen him.*

*They stare at each other. **Scully** drops the brush and box into a concrete waste bin, and then points at the lad before holding his finger to his mouth in warning. **Scully** then turns and strolls away down the side of the school.*

*The **boy** hesitates and then goes into the shadows of the shed. We hear him giggle.*

5   Inside the Probation Office

There are a few posters acknowledging the charitable work of Oxfam, the dangers of smoking, and the facilities available at the Job Centre and with the British Army. Completing the room are a filing cabinet, a battered executive's chair and a hard-backed chair, with a desk between.

*We see **Mr Flanagan,** Scully's probation officer, a man in his late twenties. He is earnest and soft. **Scully** is seated opposite to **Mr Flanagan** at a desk. **Scully** shows no reaction. **Mr Flanagan** takes a folder from a larger file. In that folder is **Scully's** school report. It is battered and torn from being kept hidden in **Scully's** pocket between terms. **Mr Flanagan** holds **Scully's** report up to him.*

Mr Flanagan: Your school report.

[**Mr Flanagan** *waits, expecting some reaction. He gets none. He looks down at the report and starts with the latest comments. He winces slightly and then goes back through the years.*

We cut back to **Scully,** *looking at* **Mr Flanagan. Scully**
*turns to the camera, and speaks straight at us. He is totally
relaxed – there is no appreciation nor 'nudge nudge' 'wink
wink'. He uses the camera like 'Whicker's World' – as his
best friend*]

Scully: He's lookin' for somethin' I'm good at. Poor sod,
it'll take him ages to find anythin'.

[*He smiles at us, and turns back to* **Mr Flanagan.** *He stares
coldly at him. We see* **Mr Flanagan** *still looking through*
Scully's *report with no joy. He looks up at* **Scully,** *smiles
cheerfully, and somewhat desperately, and looks down
again. We see* **Scully** *with a manic impersonation of* **Mr
Flanagan's** *smile on his lips. He stops it dead as we hear
and then see* **Mr Flanagan's** *sudden enthusiasm*]

Mr Flanagan: Hah-hah! [*He looks up hopefully*] It says here
that you're excellent at drama.

Scully: At wha'?

Mr Flanagan: Drama.

Scully: What's that?

Mr Flanagan: Oh come on, Francis – acting.

Scully: Actin'? I've never done none of that. Do I look as
though I wear a bra?

Mr Flanagan: Well, it says here quite categorically –

Scully: Who said so?

Mr Flanagan: A Mrs ... Heath.

Scully: Arrr, she took us for English in the second year, but
she never took us for no actin' though. [*He leans forward
and speaks to him confidentially and with confidence*] We
don't have actin' in our school – Catholic school y'see – it's
not allowed.

Mr Flanagan: [*Still looking at the report*] Not even at Christmas?

Scully: Well, there's a pantomime for the Juniors but it's last. It's not funny or nothin'. Gorra be bad hasn't it, when eight year olds throw things at y' an' try an' burn the curtains down.

Mr Flanagan: [*Getting closer to* **Scully** *each time he talks*] Last year you refused the star part in Dick Whittington.

Scully: Ah, go away will y'!

Mr Flanagan: Two years ago you turned down the male lead in Little Red Riding Hood.

Scully: Who wants to be the Big Bad Wolf?

Mr Flanagan: And three years ago you *were* in the school pantomime.

[*He looks up at* **Scully,** *who has leant forward himself as if to look at the report. We see that* **Mr Flanagan** *is reading this information off a letter from the school*]

Mr Flanagan: Snow White and the Seven Dwarfs.

Scully: Never heard of it. What is it – a sex film?

Mr Flanagan: You were Happy.

Scully: No I wasn't, I was fed-up, same as everyone else.

Mr Flanagan: But you were one of the dwarfs.

Scully: [*Straight*] Nah, actually I was Snow White.

Mr Flanagan: [*Looking up and then glancing at his information*] Seriously?

[**Scully** *looks at the camera helplessly, and we cut to an insert of* **Scully** *on a school stage dressed as Snow White, with an absurd wig, two uneven and loose coconuts, heavy make-up and broom, looking down at a* **small boy** *dressed as a dwarf.* **Scully** *speaks in high-pitched stilted tones,* *folding his arms under his 'chest' like a washerwoman*]

Scully: Tell me, Grumpy, my dear, why are you always so sad?

[*We come back to reality and* **Scully** *still looking at the camera*]

Scully: I mean, y'know, can y'imagine? [*He looks back at* **Mr Flanagan,** *and speaks with a degree of sympathy*] Look, Mr Flanagan, so all right, I was a dwarf, but you're wastin' your time with the actin', it's only for the birds, I've grown up now. I've told Mrs Heath the same – I'm not interested.

[*We see* **Mr Flanagan** *adopt a more tight-lipped, aggressive tone briefly. His psychology textbooks have indicated that this is sometimes a good idea. He closes and throws down the school report and letter.* **Scully** *stares at him*]

Mr Flanagan: *Come on.* [*There is no answer*] Are you going to dribble your life away, throw all your talents down the drain? That is, if you really have got any.

Scully: I've got *talent!*

Mr Flanagan: Tell me about it then.

[*There is a pause. For the first time* **Scully** *is not at ease*]

Scully: . . . Nah, you'd laugh. People usually do.

Mr Flanagan: No really, you can tell me anything.

Scully: What is this – confession?

Mr Flanagan: You can tell me anything in confidence, Francis, anything – providing, of course, it isn't a criminal offence.

[**Scully** *turns straight to the camera, away from the close attentions of* **Mr Flanagan**]

Scully: Sometimes y'know, he's so close to y', you can see the blackheads in his chin. [*He turns back*] Can I go now? I've just remembered, it's double physics this afternoon and I don't like missin' dou–

Mr Flanagan: You can go when you've told me what you think you're good at.

Scully: [*He pauses, then breathes out as he says the first two words*] Yeah, well, I wanna be a professional footballer, don't I?

[**Scully** *looks away from* **Mr Flanagan,** *then quickly back to see his reaction.* **Mr Flanagan** *looks away himself, then looks back at* **Scully** *just after* **Scully** *looks at him. Both look, as* **Scully** *looks at the camera, as if daring us to laugh or question*]

Scully: What are you lookin' at?

[*He holds his belligerent look until he hears* **Dalglish's** *voice*]

Dalglish: So you want to be a footballer, son?

[**Scully** *slumps slightly in his chair, and glances towards* **Mr Flanagan.** *In his place we see* **Kenny Dalglish** *looking at* **Scully** *with genuine quiet interest, leaning forward, in club suit and tie.* **Scully** *looks back at us, and speaks quietly*]

Scully: I suppose I'm going to have tell y'. I've got this problem, y'see – no really – what it is is that I keep seein' things – but it's not like, y'know, havin' day-dreams or imaginin' things – like goin' like that – [*He flicks his fingers and points towards* **Mr Flanagan.** *We see in his place, dressed in his cloth cap, a 'P.G. Tips' monkey, reading* **Scully's** *report. We come back to* **Scully**] – anyone can do that, and I do it all the time. But what's really worryin' me is that I haven't got any ... control over seeing Kenny

Dalglish. I haven't. He just keeps bein' there. [*He shakes his head and looks away, half laughs and glances back at us. He speaks flatly*] . . . do you think I might be in love?

[*We see that* **Mr Flanagan** *is looking rapidly through* **Scully's** *report. He looks up*]

Mr Flanagan: It . . . it doesn't say too much here about your footballing . . . abilities.

Scully: [*Standing*] It wouldn't, would it? Not with our P.E. teacher. He thinks a left-winger's somethin' t'do with the Labour Party.

Mr Flanagan: I do not wish to hear . . .

Scully: There's only one decent teacher, and that's Steve. He's going to . . .

Mr Flanagan: [*A severe warning*] I think that is more than enough, Scully!

Scully: But I've just come to the good bit. [*Pause*] So you don't want to hear about Steve then?

Mr Flanagan: No. [*We see* **Scully** *shake his head, defeated*] Be that as it may, I would like to bring you back to drama.

Scully: You'd need a ball and chain to bring me back there, pal.

Mr Flanagan: Mr Flanagan.

Scully: Yeah, all right. Can I go now? . . . *Mr* Flanagan.

Mr Flanagan: [*It is his turn to sigh*] Yes, you can go now. [*While* **Scully** *makes for the door,* **Mr Flanagan** *continues to speak to him*] Back to double physics. And make sure your attendance improves.

[**Scully** *gets to the door and reaches for the doorknob*]

Mr Flanagan: Francis.

[**Scully** *turns. He glances at the camera, and mutters to us*]

Scully: Here it comes – 'Thought for the Day'

Mr Flanagan: About the football, you know, don't build your hopes up, the failure rate is –

Scully: [*Exasperated*] So everyone keeps tellin' me!

[**Scully** *turns away, and we hear* **Kenny Dalglish**]

Dalglish: But it's important you know that, son.

[*We see* **Scully** *leaning his head against the door, his hand resting between his head and the door. He turns around and sees* **Dalglish** *again, at the desk, looking at him.* **Scully** *turns to us*]

Scully: See what I mean?

[*He rests his head back against the door again. We focus on* **Scully** *as* **Dalglish** *continues to speak*]

Dalglish: Dreams alone aren't enough –

[**Scully** *finally peeps almost from under his arm as* **Dalglish** *stops, and all we see is a perplexed* **Mr Flanagan** *staring at* **Scully. Scully** *visibly sags and reaches for the door handle once more.*

We see **Scully** *from the waiting room as he opens the Probation Office door, and looks towards the far corner of the waiting room. He closes the door behind him*]

6   Inside the waiting room

We now see the far corner of the waiting room. We see **Joey Kelly** *and* **Mooey Morgan. Kelly** *is a member of the remedial department of the comprehensive school. He has a frightened and bewildered* **Mooey** *up against the corner of the* *wall. As* **Scully** *closes the door behind him and enters the waiting room,* **Kelly** *turns quickly to see who it is. He eases his grip on* **Mooey** *then sees it is only* **Scully**. *He turns back to* **Mooey**.

Kelly: All right Scull. [*He laughs*] Hey come here, y'll like this.

[*He laughs again. We now see him flick his cigarette lighter close to* **Mooey's** *hair.* **Mooey** *tries to escape through the wall. He fails and yelps*]

Kelly: Go ahead, soft kecks, sing y' song.

[*He thrusts his lighter at* **Mooey** *who yelps and starts 'singing'*]

Mooey: 'Light my fire, come on baby, light my fire . . . light my fire . . .' Erm, er I don't know any more.

Kelly: That'll do. [*He lights* **Mooey's** *hair up. It singes*] Wanna go?

[**Kelly** *offers* **Scully** *the lighter.* **Mooey** *tries to put the remains of his hair out on the back wall.* **Scully** *is advancing*]

Scully: Leave him alone, Kelly.

Kelly: Wha'?

Scully: Deaf as well as daft, hey?

Kelly: But –

Scully: I said leave him alone.

Kelly: But he's only a looney from the silly school.

Mooey: Er no, I'm not, I'm just a bit slow.

[**Kelly** *turns back and flicks and thrusts the lighter at him again*]

Mooey: 'Light my fire, come on baby . . .'

Scully: [*Grabbing hold of* **Kelly's** *hand*] I won't tell you again.

Kelly: Get off!

[**Kelly** *tries to shake* **Scully** *free. He pushes at* **Scully** *who grabs him and gives him a first-rate, first-hand demonstration of the wonders of unarmed combat. It is over in a second – or three; and* **Scully** *finishes up by hurling and spinning* **Kelly** *towards the opposite side of the room exactly as* **Mr Flanagan** *opens his room door*]

Mr Flanagan: Next please!

[**Kelly** *flies in through the doorway and out of sight. We hear a crash of chairs and filing cabinets and* **Kelly**. **Mr Flanagan** *looks into his room, and then looks at* **Scully**. **Scully** *points quietly at* **Mooey**, *feels his muscles and whistles.* **Mooey** *looks aggrieved, and turns to* **Scully**]

Mooey: But that's not fair, Scull, I was next.

[**Scully** *grins as the puzzled* **Mr Flanagan** *goes into his room and closes his door*]

7   A road

We see **Scully** *and* **Mooey** *walking along the road.* **Scully** *is moving at a fast pace and* **Mooey** *is scurrying to keep up.*

Mooey: ... an' ... an' er, the ball dropped just right, Scull, an' I hit in on the trolley.

Scully: Volley.

Mooey: Er yeah, that as well – an' er, it went right in the top corner of the net, goalie beaten all the way ... Yis! [*He holds his hand up in salute*]

Scully: [*Miles away*] Cracker that, Moo. Did y' win?

Mooey: [*Uneasily*] Er . . . no, we er lost one-nil . . . But er, their team manager said it was the best goal he'd –

Scully: Mooey, listen – I want to ask you something –

Mooey: I'd like to lend you some money, Scull, but I haven't got any.

Scully: No, it's not that. What I want to know is . . . what would you say if I told you I kept seeing Kenny Dalglish?

Mooey: Er, I think I'd ask y' if I could meet him as well.

Scully: But . . . what would you say to me if I told you I kept seeing him and he wasn't there?

Mooey: [*He gets a little worried, and edges slightly away from* **Scully**] Er, I'd say . . . er, I er . . . I'd say 'goodbye', Scull . . .

[*We fade on them as they approach* **Scully's** *school and* **Mooey** *keeps peeping cautiously at* **Scully**]

8   Inside the school canteen

We see **Scully** *and* **Mooey** *tucked away in the corner at a table for four. With them are* **Mad Dog** *and* **Snotty Dog. Snotty Dog** *is the younger of the two.* **Scully** *can survey the room from his chair, which backs onto the wall.* **Mooey** *is alongside him, his head very much down.*

Mad Dog: That dinner woman with the dermatitis recognized y', y'know, Moo.

Mooey: [*Twitching and looking from beneath his eyebrows*] I know.

Mad Dog: She knows y' don't go to our school anymore. Y've had it now.

Mooey: No I haven't. It's er . . . all right. She asked me if I was still here. [*He nods as if that is the conclusion of the argument*]

Mad Dog: And what did y' say?

Mooey: I er, told her I must be here, 'cos I er, knew for a fact I wasn't anywhere else. Otherwise she would've had to shout to talk to me.

[**Mad Dog** *and* **Snotty Dog** *look at* **Mooey** *and then at each other. They are baffled by* **Mooey**'*s intellect and awareness of time and space*]

Scully: Nah, no sweat, y' just another plate an' a pair of dirty hands to them. Y' sound as a pound, don't – [*He glances up*] Look out, *Mrs Heath!*

[*We cut quickly to* **Mrs Heath** *marching through the dining hall. She is a middle-aged, middle-class, well-dressed attractive woman with silver hair and a Capstan Full Strength in her hand . . . We cut back to the dinner table.* **Scully** *has 'gone'. We see* **Mooey** *looking confused and then under the table. He begins to kneel down to hide as well. When he is finally out of sight, we see his hand come back up and take his pudding dish down with him as well. We see* **Snotty Dog** *and* **Mad Dog** *as they look up and smile with innocence and difficulty*]

Mrs Heath: Get up, Francis, come on, stop playing soft ollies.

[*We see* **Scully** *get up as* **Mrs Heath** *lights another cigarette off the one she already has, which is only half smoked*]

Scully: I, er, just dropped me spoon, Mrs Heath, y'know, couldn't find it anywhere.

[**Mrs Heath** *studies the ceiling. The others study it too*]

Scully: It won't be up there . . .

Mrs Heath: No, I was just looking for flying pigs. [*She smiles sweetly at him, and drops her old cigarette on the floor*] Now I had Mr Flanagan on the phone before dinner –

[*We see* **Mooey's** *hand sneaking out from beneath the table to take the cigarette off the floor. As he does so,* **Mrs Heath** *stands on the cigarette and his hand. He yelps, nearly silently*]

Mrs Heath: Seems a very committed young man, highly concerned about your welfare. [**Scully** *scowls*] Talked to me about the possibilities of using your dramatic talents. [**Scully** *looks pained*] I'm holding auditions for this year's pantomime next week – I expect you to be there.

Scully: Array Miss. [*We see* **Mad Dog** *and* **Snotty Dog**, *heads down, as they snigger at* **Scully**. *He sees them as well*] I'll never make an actor, Miss – I don't buy me clothes from Ladies Underwear.

Mrs Heath: [*Angrily*] Don't be so damned childish!

[*We see the few stragglers from the end of school dinner turn and look. One of them is a beautiful* **black girl**. **Scully** *looks at her very quickly, and turns away*]

Mrs Heath: You have a lot of ability, more than you yourself have any concept of, boy, but you're wasting it completely, and if there's one thing I cannot stand, Francis, it's waste. Do you hear me? [*No answer*] Do you hear me?

Scully: Yes Miss.

Mrs Heath: Right, good, I expect to see you there.

Scully: I'm sorry Miss, but y'know, I'd rather play football. Honest.

Mrs Heath: Next Tuesday, a three o'clock call.

Scully: I'd call it a day if I were you.

Mrs Heath: You'll be there. [*She smiles*] One way or another. [*She turns to go, walks a few paces, and then stops*] You can come out now, Mooey, I've gone.

Mooey: Er, all right, er, thanks Miss . . .

[*As* **Mrs Heath** *marches away swirled in smoke, and as* **Mooey** *rises from beneath the table sucking his fingers,* **Snotty Dog** *starts to collect the plates, and* **Scully** *again focuses slyly on the* **black girl**]

Snotty Dog: [*To* **Scully**] Er, would you care to pass y' plate Mr Brando?

[**Scully** *looks at* **Snotty Dog** *and* **Mad Dog**, *and then at his spoon in his semolina and jam. He looks up stone-faced at* **Snotty Dog** – *then flicks a large dollop of pudding into* **Snotty Dog***'s face*]

9   A school corridor

We see **Scully** *and* **Mooey** *walking along a corridor together, side by side. As they do so, the* **black girl** *again appears, walking past them.* **Scully** *stops for a second and looks at her going down the corridor. He then begins to catch up with* **Mooey**. *As he approaches a doorway, a hand comes out from the doorway and jerks* **Scully** *violently on the arm, so that he disappears into the room almost cartoon-like.*

We see **Mooey** *carrying on walking. He hasn't seen a thing.*

10   Inside the caretaker's room at school

We see **Scully** *up against the wall in the caretaker's room. He is pinned there by a wild-eyed, fang-toothed Mr Moss –* **Dracula**

*In the background is Mr Banks, his assistant caretaker, quietly displaying the worst-fitting, loudest-clicking set of false teeth outside the Third World – '***Castanets***'.*

Dracula: It was you, wasn't it!

Castanets: Wasn't it.

Scully: Wah'? [**Dracula** *shakes him*] Gerroff!

Dracula: You did it all right, I can tell.

Scully: I will do something in a minute if you don't let go.

[**Dracula** *lets go, reluctantly. He points to his side, but won't look himself. We see a moped. Painted on the side, with some skill, is a picture of Dracula in a cape.* **Scully** *can't help grinning*]

Dracula: I told you, I told you. I knew it was you. [*He grabs hold of him*] I'm taking you to the headmaster.

Castanets: The headmaster. [*Click click, slobber*]

Scully: [*He pushes* **Dracula** *away*] You're takin' me nowhere. Not till you've got proof.

Dracula: All right, where were you between the hours of eleven o'clock and the end of morning school? Hey? Hey come on, answer me.

Castanets: Me . . . Him.

Scully: [*Grinning*] I've got an alibi, govner.

Dracula: A likely story.

Castanets: Story. [**Dracula** *looks at him.* **Castanets** *bangs his broom and teeth in support*]

Scully: No, y'see, I was with someone.

Dracula: Yeah, no doubt the pair of you did it together.

[**Castanets** *nods*]

Scully: There'll be trouble if we did – y'see I was with me probation officer.

[**Scully** *takes his appointments card out from his inside pocket. He flicks it at* **Dracula** *and* **Castanets**. **Dracula** *drops it*]

Dracula: Pick that up.

[**Castanets** *picks it up.* **Dracula** *leans over his shoulder to look. As he does so,* **Scully** *talks to the camera. He indicates . . .*]

Scully: Dracula and Castanets. School caretakers.

[*We see them from* **Scully's** *point of view as he continues to talk over and we see an insert of* **Castanets** *dressed like a flamenco dancer, his teeth acting like castanets, performing 'We're off to Sunny Spain'. Then we see* **Dracula** *dressed as Dracula, leaning on* **Castanets's** *shoulder, sinking his now monstrous fangs into the side of* **Castanets's** *bare neck*]

Scully: [*Voice over*] He's the boss – Dracula – and he's a real pain in the neck. Castanets's got the kind of teeth, every time he opens his mouth, he comes two inches nearer to y'.

[*We see* **Castanets** *giving back the card. Both caretakers are in their normal boilersuits and* **Dracula's** *fangs have subsided*]

Dracula: Yes well, we'll see about that, I'll make my own enquiries.

Castanets: Enquiries.

Dracula: And hey, be warned, don't think I don't know who you are. I know you all right, you're one of those swines always tryin' to get in the gymnasium after school. I've seen you.

Scully: Ooooh, y' talkin' about real crime now. [*He tut tuts*]

Dracula: Don't be cheeky – and don't try it. [*Working himself up into a semi-coronary situation*] You lot ought to know by now, I'm sick and tired of tellin' y', y' can't play in the gym if there's no teacher with y'. It's in the rules, it's not safe, it's more than not safe, it's dangerous. If y' fall an' break y' leg, don't come runnin' t' me, 'cos it's nothin' to do with me, I won't get the blame, so go on, clear off, and be warned!

Castanets: Yes.

[**Scully** *looks at them with a mixture of contempt and laughter. He then turns and moves towards the door*]

11   The school corridor

We see **Scully** *leave the caretaker's room, move down the corridor and turn a corner. As he does this, we see* **Mooey** *turn the far corner of the corridor, heading towards the caretaker's room. He looks lost and confused, and hesitates as he gets near. As he does so, we see the* **red-haired boy** *from the bike shed go past* **Mooey** *and towards the caretaker's office. As he reaches the doorway, a few yards from* **Mooey,** *we see the same hand reach out from the doorway and snatch the* **red-haired boy** *away. We hear* **Dracula**

Dracula: It was you, wasn't it?

[*We see* **Mooey,** *who has witnessed this scene, backing away*]

12   Inside the general science lab

We see **Steve** *– Mr Stephens – in the science lab, sitting at the demonstration table at the front. He is man in his late forties,* *with a limp and the kind of warm lived-in features that give a quiet aura of assurance and kindness. The bell is going for the end of the lesson, the last of the afternoon. Most of the class are leaving the room. We are left with* **Scully, Mad Dog,** *and several other boys, one of whom we recognize later as* **Brian Bignall.** *The others push* **Scully** *forward. He hesitates, then speaks.*

Scully: Steve. Sir.

Steve: Yes?

Scully: It's, er . . . we just wondered if y' could do us a favour.

Steve: I can only say no. [*Misses a beat*] No. [*Then he grins and shuffles in his pocket for his pipe*]

Scully: It's the er, gymnasium, Steve. We want to have a game of five-a-side in there, but you know, like, *now*, after school, but we can't.

Steve: Because?

Mad Dog: [*Flaring*] What do you mean 'because'? You know why because, because of that Count Dracula, he won't let us, and none of the other teachers'll even . . . even . . . they won't do nothin', I'm goin' to kill them, I am, I'll kill them all dead, I will, I'll . . .

[**Scully** *leans over and clamps his hand over* **Mad Dog's** *mouth*]

Scully: Just an hour, what do you say? Till five o'clock.

Scully: [*Looks at his watch*] You'd better go and get changed then, hadn't you?

[*The others run off, quietly delighted.* **Scully** *stays where he is*]

Scully: When's the big day, Steve?

Steve: [*Genuinely puzzled*] What big day? I'm already married.

Scully: You know, Blackburn Rovers. Your old club – my big chance . . . me trial.

Steve: You weren't the only boy in the room when I said that, Francis.

Scully: Y' meant me though didn't y'?

Steve: You're a very useful player, very useful indeed, but I was talking to the whole team. And it wasn't a promise, kidder.

Scully: But I'm the best player . . . I am, aren't I? You said . . .

Steve: I said that if you're good enough, if you're dedicatd enough, if you look after yourself enough –

Scully: You'll take us to Blackburn Rovers for a trial. That's what y' said. And I am. I'm all those things.

[**Steve** *leans forward across the desk and lifts a loose cigarette out of* **Scully's** *pocket and holds it out to him*]

Scully: I'm keepin' it for me Mam. [*He takes it back, but doesn't look up*]

Steve: Go and get changed.

Scully: But –

Steve: Go and get changed and show me.

[**Steve** *smiles at* **Scully** *– in dismissal.* **Scully** *hesitates and then goes towards the door. We fade on* **Steve's** *frown*]

13   A school corridor

We see the others running towards the gymnasium. They turn into the corridor leading to it.

As soon as they have gone, we see **Mooey** *walking past, just* *missing them, and as soon as* **Mooey** *has moved up the corridor and away,* **Scully** *enters from the opposite end of the corridor.* **Scully** *walks along towards the corridor leading to the gym. As soon as he vanishes,* **Mooey** *comes back, just missing* **Scully** *again.*

14   Inside the gymnasium

We see the gymnasium. We see **Steve** *organizing the boys into two teams of five to pick up bean bags – two boys at a time from each team.* **Scully** *is racing against* **Mad Dog**, *just beating him despite* **Mad Dog's** *death threats. We hear* **Steve** *pushing them on.*

Mad Dog: I'll kill y'. I will, if you beat me, I'll kill y' . . .

Steve: Come on, come on, quicker on the turn, turn, *turn* . . . shut up, O'Gorman . . . you're slowing, Scully, you're slowing, faster . . .

[*We see* **Scully**, *nearly knackered, pushing himself. As he does so, we see him looking towards* **Steve**. *And in* **Steve's** *place is* **Kenny Dalglish** *in a red track suit, pushing* **Scully** *on*]

Dalglish: Come on son, come on, the first five yards, go go go, move yourself, Scully, move, back again back again, again *again*!

[**Scully** *finishes his part of the race and slows down. Then he looks up half expectantly for* **Dalglish**. *All he sees is* **Steve**. *He grimaces and puts his head down again.*

We see the lads playing five-a-side, giving everything. We see a move that is finished by **Scully** *thumping in a volley. We see his face drop as he runs back. He glances at* **Steve**, *who is sitting quietly in the corner of the gym with his bad leg resting on the second chair.* **Scully** *then looks away again,* *in the direction of the gym door. He scowls, but there is no fear nor panic.*

We see **Dracula** *and* **Castanets** *in normal clothing through the separate windows of the gym doors.* **Dracula** *is staring wildly and happily, nose jammed against the window.* **Castanets** *is more distantly framed against the second window. He is holding a mop and bucket close to the window. We cannot see anything else.*

We come back to **Scully** *as we hear shouts from the other boys. The game is in motion again and the ball is bobbing about near* **Scully***. He ignores it.*

We cut back to **Dracula** *and* **Castanets***.* **Dracula** *grabs hold of the gym door nearest* **Castanets***, and pulls it towards* **Castanets** *viciously. We see* **Castanets's** *mop handle make a neat little hole in the gym door window.* **Dracula** *turns for a second, fangs drawn]*

Dracula: Stay there! *[Coupled with the sound of breaking glass. This brings everyone to halt. The boys all look across towards the gym doorway]* Out, go on, get out, no teacher, clear off right now. *[Then he points]* All except you. *[We see* **Scully***]*

Scully: No chance. Shove off, Dracula, go an' rob a blood bank. But first of all take a good look around y'self.

Dracula: *[Ignoring his offer]* Don't talk to me like that. I've got a position here, now –

Scully: Go an' position y' bad breath somewhere else *[triumphantly]* 'cos we've got a teacher!

Steve: Scully. *Scully*! Shut up and grow up!

[We see **Dracula** *double take and then stand back in amazement. We see* **Scully** *back away and mutter to himself]*

Dracula: Oh well, even better, just the very man. Oh yes.

[*He turns back towards the gym doors*] I've got bigger fish to fry than playing in the gym without a teacher . . .

Steve: [*Flatly*] I am a teacher.

[**Dracula** *reaches out into the corridor smiling happily. Going into the corridor briefly, he grabs hold of and half brings in the wrong person –* **Castanets**. *But then we see the small* **red-haired boy** *being dragged into the gymnasium by the scruff of the neck, having previously been hidden beneath the gym door windows*]

Dracula: Right, go on, tell y' teacher, tell him who painted my moped, go on, tell him what you've told me.

[*We see the* **red-haired boy**, *plainly scared and hesitant. He looks around the room. He has no friends there. He looks up at* **Dracula**]

Red-haired boy: I wanna plead the – the fifth commandment –

Steve: Let go of the boy, please.

Dracula: But it was him, that one, Scully. He did it.

Scully: I wouldn't waste the paint. [*Some laughter.* **Dracula** *goes to grab hold of* **Scully** *by his football shirt*]

Scully: Leave me neck alone!

Steve: Mr Moss. Remember this: you're a caretaker, your job is to take care, and I rather think that you should. Meanwhile, I'll take care of this matter.

Dracula: But –

Steve: Thank you.

Scully: [*Smirking*] Lost again hey, Dracula. Fangs ain't what they used to be.

Steve: Francis, go and get dressed and wait outside my room. *Now*.

Scully: Who me? *Me*? What for?

Steve: Because you're out of order – now do as I say.

Scully: Who's side are you on, hey Steve – who's side are you on?

Steve: Wait outside my room.

Scully: [*Marching away*] Fat chance. [**Dracula** *laughs as* **Scully** *passes*]

Steve: Scully!

[**Scully** *ignores* **Steve** *and approaches the doors. We see* **Castanets** *peering through the broken window.* **Scully** *pushes at the door angrily, and inevitably* **Castanets'** *broom goes straight through that window too.* **Scully** *barges past him and away, and* **Castanets** *looks in disbelief at the shattered windows*]

15   A school corridor

We see **Scully** *slam out of the gym and march off. He goes towards the corridor leading to the front exit of the school, turns into the corridor and stops in his tracks. We see coming towards him, at the far end of the corridor, and deep in discussion,* **Mrs Heath** *and* **Mr Flanagan***, in a swirl of* **Mrs Heaths's** *cigarette smoke.* **Scully** *retreats towards the fire exit and tries to open it. He fails. He can hear the voices of* **Mr Flanagan** *and* **Mrs Heath** *approaching.*

16   Outside the school

We see, from outside, the fire exit burst open. We see, in the follow through, that **Scully** *has kicked it open – and knocked*

Mooey *tumbling over. Inevitably,* **Mooey** *has been sitting against the door waiting for* **Scully**. **Scully** *picks him up, in passing, and moves quickly away.*

Mooey: [*Scuttling after him*] Er, what's the matter, Scull?

Scully: Ah, everyone's gettin' on me back, Moo. [**Mooey** *looks briefly at* **Scully's** *back*] ... Soddin' Steve of all people, Dracula ... Mrs Heath ... me probation officer ... and then there's the fact that nobody ever believes me!

Mooey: I believe y' Scull, I always believe you ... Er, what is it that er, they don't believe?

Scully: They think I painted Dracula on the caretaker's bike.

Mooey: Yes! I believe it. I knew you'd do something like that.

Scully: [*Looks at him and smiles*] Yeah, well.

[*We hear voices from the distance.* **Scully** *and* **Mooey** *turn around. Approaching from the fire exit to the school are* **Dracula, Castanets, Mrs Heath, Mr Flanagan** *and* **Steve**]

Dracula: Hey, you, Scully, come here you. I haven't finished with you yet!

Mr Flanagan: [*Barely heard*] Francis, just a moment ...

[**Steve** *and* **Mrs Heath** *are also shouting to* **Scully**]

Steve: Come on Francis. Crying out loud.

[**Scully** *looks at* **Mooey**. **Mrs Heath, Mr Flanagan** *and* **Steve** *start to move to* **Scully**. **Dracula** *attempts to start his moped*]

Scully: Aye, aye, here's the cavalry.

Mooey: Er, what do you mean, Scully?

Scully: Well you know in cowboy films when the cavalry comes over the hill?

Mooey: [*With enthusiasm*] Yis!

Scully: The only trouble is we're the Red Indians!

[*Immediately, we see* **Scully** *and* **Mooey** *as Indians. They race off down the road, pursued by* **Mrs Heath**, **Mr Flanagan**, **Steve**, **Dracula** *and* **Castanets** – *who are dressed in cavalry uniform and mounted on horseback*]

Episode 2

A happy family: the Scullys. Back row: *Mrs Scully (Val Lilley), Francis (Andrew Schofield), and Tony (Peter Christian).* In the foreground: *Arthur (Jimmy Gallagher), Gran (Jean Boht) and Henry (Elvis Costello).*

Episode 2

---

1 A road

We see **Scully** *and* **Mooey** *walking towards* **Mooey's** *house.*

Scully: Go on, Moo, you get your ball hey, it's miles to ours, and we'll have a practice in the park. I'll give you some tips.

Mooey: I don't like horse racin'.

Scully: About football. Tips about football. What to do an' that. You can go in goal to start with. [*Winks at him*]

Mooey: That's not fair. I always go in goal. They even make me go in goal when I'm playin' cricket.

[*We see the beautiful* **black girl** *from episode one as she walks towards* **Scully** *and* **Mooey**, *before going into the pathway of a house a couple of doors away from* **Mooey's** *house.* **Scully** *talks as he sees her and as they reach* **Mooey's** *pathway*]

2 Outside Mooey's house

Scully: All right, I'll go goalie first. Three goals in.

Mooey: Yis! You'll be in goal f'ages.

[**Mooey's** *door opens and we see* **Marie Morgan**, *the same* *age as* **Scully** *but trying to look twenty-seven. She is fatally attracted to leather and mascara. She is leaning 'seductively' all over the doorway, smoking a cigarette as* **Scully** *focuses on her*]

Marie: Why hello, Francis. What a big boy you're becoming. It's so nice to see you in long trousers . . .

Scully: Give order will y', Marie, we're the same age.

Marie: Never!

Scully: The only reason you haven't noticed is 'cos y' haven't been to school since the start of the Juniors.

Marie: What's it like?

Scully: School?

Marie: No, becoming a big boy . . .

[**Scully** *glances at the camera and then looks at* **Mooey,** *who looks puzzled.* **Scully** *attempts bravado with* **Marie** – *he advances towards her*]

Scully: Do you wanna find out, girl?

Marie: [*Laughing*] How would I do that?

Mooey: [*In stage whisper*] Be careful, Scull, she might kiss y'.

Scully: I'll have to show you, won't I?

[**Scully** *leans against the door frame, very close to her . . . and then closer. She is standing on the step, so she simpers above him as he looks up at her, trying to be hard and cool. This continues for some time*]

Mooey: Ah this is borin'. [*He walks between them, separating them, and goes into the house*]

Marie: Well go on then, show me. Who knows, I might have been missing something.

[**Scully** *moves close to her again, and rests his arm against the door frame. We hear* **Mooey** *from inside the house*]

Mooey: [*Inside*] Have you seen me balls, Marie? [**Marie** *tries hard not to giggle, but gives up;* **Scully** *scowls and moves back.* **Mooey** *arrives at the door*] Have you though?

Marie: Not lately.

Mooey: [*Inside*] Oh. The dog must have them. [*Shouting*] Cripple, here y'are boy, come on, Cripple . . .

Marie: [*To* **Scully**] Ahhhh, going to the park for a nice game of football. And a sarsparilla afterwards. Wearin' your shorts?

Scully: Behave y'self, Marie. And it's not just a game of football. It's a practice session.

Marie: You'll never be perfect, but you might pass an afternoon . . .

Scully: Is that an invitation? [*He gets closer to her yet again. She smiles encouragingly. We hear a dog snarling violently and* **Mooey** *yelping. They are ignored.* **Scully** *is very near to her. She looks over his head slightly.* **Scully** *has his arm just above the doorframe she is leaning against. He leans towards her. This time . . . we see a tattooed hand tap him on the shoulder.* **Scully** *turns around and looks up. And up. A* **Giant** *of about twenty – age and weight in stones – towers over him, dressed to overkill in leather and tattooes.* **Scully** *turns back to* **Marie**] . . . So erm, me Mam said to tell y' that our Vera'll definitely be in the Parish Club at –

[**Marie** *walks past him and accompanies the heavyweight down the path. She looks back once at the gate and purses her lips*]

Marie: Have a nice game, Francis.

[**Scully** *stares at her*]

Scully: Didn't fancy her anyway . . .

[**Mooey** *appears at the doorway with a beachball, the same size as a football*]

Scully: [*To* **Mooey**] Plannin' a holiday?

Mooey: The dog's ate the caseball, Scull.

3   A park

We see the park. We see the Lord Mayor's car parked by the gates, the **driver** *having a sly smoke, blowing the smoke out of the window. We see the* **Lord Mayor** *at the edge of the park. He is holding a spade and bending down, smiling for a solitary* **photographer** *from the local weekly newspaper. The proceedings are being watched by* **Scully** *and* **Mooey**.

We see that two dozen new saplings have been planted. We hear desultory ironic applause, and wolf whistles, and jeers. The **Lord Mayor** *scowls and gives the spade back without looking. He gives it to* **Mooey**, *who has edged closer and closer and is now staring at him.* **Mooey** *promptly gives it to* **Scully**, *and the* **gardener** *grabs it off* **Scully** *as* **Scully** *considers going home. The* **Lord Mayor** *hurries away towards his car.*

We now see that his audience, apart from **Scully** *and* **Mooey**, *has been two women with shopping and a gang of kids coming home from school. One of the women (***Mrs 'Crackers' Leigh** *dressed in a bright green coat, pushing a big basket of groceries) comes closer to inspect the labels on the trees.*

Scully: What was all that in aid of?

Mooey: He's er, been buryin' trees, Scull. Diggin' holes an' buryin' them.

Scully: Oh I'm sorry, I didn't know it was a funeral.

Mooey: Oh no, they're not dead. He was only buryin' them.

Mrs Leigh: It's Plant-a-Tree Week, y' soft gets.

Scully: Pardon, madam?

Mrs Leigh: It's to make the estate look nicer, so you can look at them and appreciate them and get something out of them.

Scully: They wanna plant some factories then.

Mrs Leigh: [*Walking away*] Communists.

Mooey: I'm not, I'm a Catholic.

Mrs Leigh: Soft gets.

Mooey: That's more like it.

Scully: [*Playing with the saplings, tugging gently at one of them*] Doing anything tonight, Moo?

Mooey: Er no. Shall I bring me spade?

[**Scully** *grins admiringly at* **Mooey** *who grins back and winks hugely*]

Scully: Nah, one tug an' they'll come up.

[**Mooey** *turns and throws the ball up in the air, and closes his eyes and tries to kick it over the Welsh mountains: he misses completely, and falls flat on his face.* **Scully** *laughs, looks away, and then suddenly joins* **Mooey** *flat on the floor*]

Mooey: Did you miss it as well, Scull?

[**Scully** *points towards the roadway, seen between the saplings, etc. We see* **Mr Flanagan** *and his briefcase walking along the road.*

They wait till he has gone past. **Scully** *shakes his head, then gets up, and flicks the ball away, towards the football pitch further into the park.* **Mooey** *gets up and follows him.*]

They pass **Mrs Leigh**. *We see* **Scully** *dribbling the ball on towards one of the goals. He turns and knocks the ball to* **Mooey**, *who stands still, and waits carefully for the ball to arrive. He puts his foot on it and stops it, and then looks up to see if* **Scully** *is impressed.*

We see **Scully** *glance at us.* **Mooey** *shouts and kicks the ball back.* **Scully** *controls the ball, and shouts as he does so*]

Scully: One-two, Moo!

[*He looks up. We see* **Dalglish** *where* **Mooey** *was, already running.* **Scully** *registers surprise for a second. He looks down, sees a real caseball, and stares at it.* **Dalglish** *shouts for the ball.* **Scully** *hits it just in front of him.* **Dalglish** *hits it back promptly in front of* **Scully** *for him to run onto.* **Scully** *looks towards goal. He sees a figure in green, looking like* **Bruce Grobbelaar**. **Scully** *pushes the ball forward, then hits a ferocious drive.* **Grobbelaar** *gets a hand to it as he dives, but is still beaten.* **Scully** *turns victorious, hand in air, towards* **Dalglish**. *We, and he, see* **Mooey** *instead of* **Dalglish**, *and* **Mooey** *is looking from behind his hand towards the goalmouth.* **Scully** *looks back. We see* **Mrs Leigh** *spreadeagled amongst her shopping between the goalposts*]

Mrs Leigh: You stupid soft gets . . .

4   Scully's house

We see **Scully** *at his doorway, opening the front door. He turns and glances at the camera, as if unsure about whether he wants us to see the contents of the house. He shrugs and goes in. We see his* **Gran** *on the stairs, holding her head.*

Gran: Oh me soddin' head . . .

Scully: [*To the camera*] Me Gran. She's had ale.

[**Scully** *carries on into the back kitchen, past the living room. We see* **Henry** *in the back kitchen, dressed normally apart from his British Rail hat. He is sitting on a chair by the table, with an ear plug attached to a portable cassette player. He is listening hard. As* **Scully** *talks to us, he casually opens a loaf, feels the tea pot, and starts to make some Spam sandwiches*]

Scully: [*To the camera*] Our Henry. Me mam fell down two flights of steps when she was carryin' him, and then me dad dropped him on his head walkin' out of Mill Road Maternity. The only thing he's ever cared about in his life was his train set. The finest train set in the whole of Liverpool. Till it blew up last New Year's Eve.

[**Scully** *leans over and pulls the plug out of the cassette player. We hear train noises and a station master's voice announcing the late arrival of the Euston train.* **Henry** *says nothing, and puts the plug back in.* **Scully** *continues to make sandwiches as his* **Gran** *enters the back kitchen – slowly*]

Gran: Ooooooh God in Heaven. [*She sits down hard and holds her head*] . . . I can't take it like I used to be able to take it once . . . Make me something to eat, Francis, there's a good lad . . . [*He starts making another sandwich*] Oh aye, before I forget, there was someone t' see you before . . . wanted to see you an' y'mam. [*She is now talking from between her folded arms on the table*]

Scully: I wish Joe Fagin'd leave me alone. I'll sign for Liverpool when I'm good an' ready, not before. These things can't be rushed.

Gran: No, it wasn't him. He said his name was Flanagan. [**Scully** *groans*] I asked him where Allen was but he didn't understand. He . . . he said he'd call back another time . . .

[**Scully** *pours a cup of tea for himself as* **Gran** *finishes. He puts her sandwich by her head as she slumps forward. He sits down at the table, facing his* **Gran***, and goes to bite his sandwich. Just as he does so, his* **Gran** *stumbles out of her slumbers long enough to take her false teeth out and place them on the table, before slumping down again. Soon she begins snoring.* **Scully** *looks at the teeth dripping on the table. He takes his sandwich away from his mouth, picks up his tea and stands up. He then goes out without comment. As soon as he goes out, we see* **Henry's** *hand slide across the table and grab the sandwich. As he is about to eat it we see* **Scully** *pop his head back around the corner of the doorway, and catch* **Henry***. He grins at him.* **Henry** *refuses even to accept that* **Scully** *is there, except to push the sandwich in his lap. Finally, he brings the sandwich up to his mouth, slowly and suspiciously.*

We see **Scully** *walking up the stairs, and reaching the room he shares with* **Arthur***, his eight-year old brother. He pushes the door open with his foot*]

5   Scully's bedroom

We see **Arthur** *dressed in a large dress, holding a handbag and wearing lipstick, make-up and curlers. He turns and smiles at* **Scully** *who shuts his eyes tight and retreats.*

We see **Scully** *coming down the stairs and approaching the living-room door. He opens the door.*

6   The living room

We see **Tony** *writing a letter, sitting on a chair, close to the television. He sees* **Scully** *and quickly shoves the letter under the cushion. He focuses on 'Jackanory'. He then glances at* **Scully***, smiles, fidgets and focuses again.*

Scully: And then there's our Tony. The Great Pretender. [*Laughs*] Goes the match of a Saturday, stands outside the Players' Entrance in his best suit, signin' autographs – at three o'clock when they kick off, he goes home. [*We come back to* **Scully**] Who's the letter to this time?

Tony: What letter?

Scully: The one y' sittin' one.

Tony: Oh that one! Mmm . . . nobody.

Scully: Nobody? Well, I hope y' not waitin' on a reply.

Tony: [*Snapping at him*] Nobody *you* know.

Scully: Will the Chelsea scout be watchin' y' play again this Sunday?

Tony: Are you being funny?

Scully: Not as funny as you last Sunday.

Tony: I haven't got a clue what you're talkin' about. Anyroad, you've got no room to talk, you're always goin' on about Blackburn Rovers – and I've never seen no scouts at the door f' you yet.

Scully: But I'm only sixteen, there's plenty of time for me. You're twenty-four.

Tony: Nineteen.

Scully: You're even lyin' about your age now.

[*As* **Scully** *laughs at* **Tony,** *we hear the front door being opened.* **Tony** *suddenly digs into his pocket and takes some five pound notes out, puts one back in his pocket and stuffs the rest into his back pocket. He just makes it as* **Mrs Scully** *enters the room, bustling in with her shopping. A woman of enormous nervous energy and vitality, she is to this house what the captain should have been to the Titanic*]

Tony: [*With false joy*] All right Mam, what's for tea? I'm starvin'.

Mrs Scully: Wishful thinkin' an' pie in the sky till you give me some money, y' idle sod.

Tony: It's, er, me first week. Y' don't get paid on y' first week.

Mrs Scully: The money lender. I told y' to see him. There's one in every works. Even the Corpy.

Tony: He'd only give me five, with me bein' new there.

Mrs Scully: That'll do.

Tony: I'll give y' three, Mam.

Mrs Scully: Y'll give me four or y'll be lookin' f' digs.

Tony: Array Mam, what about me? I've got to live y' know.

Mrs Scully: Is that what y' call it?

[*She offers* **Tony** *a pound note out of her bag. He reluctantly takes it, gives her the five pound note and sulks at the television. As he does so, we see* **Gran** *enter the living room, still half asleep, being helped by* **Henry** *with his cassette and ear plug.* **Gran** *is holding her head with one hand and her teeth with the other. She walks past* **Mrs Scully** *and gives her the teeth, then drops onto the couch, moaning*]

Mrs Scully: What's the matter with you?

Gran: I had too much to drink at the funeral . . .

Mrs Scully: Where's Arthur?

Scully: In my room lookin' pretty.

Mrs Scully: [*Sighs*] The sooner he grows out of that the better. It's costin' me a fortune in lipstick. [*She goes to sit down, then stops*] What's he wearin'?

Scully: A dozen curlers, two bottles of perfume an' y' black silk dress.

Mrs Scully: [*Storming to the doorway*] The little sod, I only ironed that this mornin' ... [*She shouts up the stairs*] Arthur, *Arthur*, get down here this minute!

Scully: I'm goin' now, Mam.

Mrs Scully: What about y' tea?

Scully: I've made myself somethin'.

Tony: I'm hungry, Mam.

Mrs Scully: [*Without looking*] Go upstairs an' eat the monkey ... [*To* **Scully**] Stay out of trouble, that's all. D'you hear me?

[**Scully** *nods as* **Arthur** *enters, proudly. He sweeps into the room*]

Arthur: What d' y' think, Mam?

Mrs Scully: Stand there where everyone can see y'. Go on. I was goin' out in that dress tonight.

[**Arthur** *stands there, unconcerned*]

Arthur: Zip me up, will y', Mam.

Mrs Scully: Sufferin' Nora, what have I done to deserve this. [*She half smiles. There is a knock on the door.* **Henry** *is nearest to the door*] See who that is, will y', Henry. [*No answer*] Henry! [*He takes the ear plug out. We hear faintly the sound of trains*] See who it is. If it's the catalogue, I'm not in.

Scully: I'm goin', Mam.

Mrs Scully: All right. But remember what I've told you before. [**Scully** *nods, and edges towards the door*] And no goin' in pubs ... and don't go near that amusement arcade ... and keep out of the cemetery ... and be in before eleven. [**Scully** *nods each time, then turns away*] An' don't go near any gangs – I don't want to fetch you from Casualty.

[**Scully** *nods again. There is now a timid knock on the*

living-room door. **Scully** *opens the door, and then closes his eyes.*

We see **Mr Flanagan**. *He steps into the room a pace or two.* **Henry** *follows him.* **Mr Flanagan** *looks around the room, and sees* **Gran** *collapsed on the couch,* **Arthur** *in a woman's black dress, unzipped at the back,* **Henry** *in his hat,* **Tony** *an inch from the television,* **Mrs Scully** *holding a set of dentures, and* **Scully** *scowling*]

Mr Flanagan: Er, Mrs Scully? I'm Mr Flanagan, Francis' probation officer.

7   The kitchen

We come back into a close-up of **Mrs Scully**, *as she speaks. We are in the back kitchen.* **Mrs Scully** *and* **Mr Flanagan** *are standing by the table.* **Mrs Scully** *has her arms folded across her chest.* **Scully** *is leaning against the draining board, head down and legs crossed.* **Mr Flanagan** *has a file in his hands.*

Mrs Scully: Well do I? [*Misses a beat*] Do I have to walk you up there at five to nine every mornin' like an infant – hold your hand and bring you back at four o'clock?

Scully: No Mam, but . . .

Mrs Scully: He'll be back in school from now on, Mr . . .

Mr Flanagan: Flanagan.

Mrs Scully: Mr Flanagan. I'll make sure of that, an' y' can tell that actin' woman –

Mr Flanagan: Mrs Heath.

Mrs Scully: Y' can tell her – any nonsense out of him, she's to let me know.

Mr Flanagan: Thank you, Mrs Scully. I can understand with Francis not having his father around to –

Mrs Scully: [*Angrily*] What's that got to do with it? Even when his dad was here, Francis wasn't where he should be – come to that, neither was his father.

Mr Flanagan: Yes well, I'm very pleased that you've . . .

Mrs Scully: Yeah, OK, now if you'll excuse me, y' know, I've got a lot to do.

[**Mr Flanagan** *has no option but to go. He turns towards the hallway*]

Mr Flanagan: [*Doubtfully*] Well, goodbye. [*He lets himself out*]

Scully: [*To* **Mrs Scully**] I suppose y' goin' to tell me I can't go out now.

[**Mrs Scully** *is throwing chips into a pan. She speaks gently*]

Mrs Scully: No. Why should I do that? What good will it do, son? You'll either sulk or sneak out anyway. [*Pause. She turns back to the cooker*] . . . Y' dad was no good, y' know that, don't y'?

Scully: Yeah, yeah, but he was a laugh, an' he was all right with me.

Mrs Scully: On the odd occasions he recognized y' . . . there's a pound in me purse if y' want it.

Scully: Nah, y' all right. [*He moves to the door, and mumbles*] Thanks anyway . . .

Mrs Scully: Fair enough, I'll put it towards me ticket money.

Scully: Ticket money? What for?

Mrs Scully: The pantomime, Francis. Oooh, you'd make a lovely Prince Charming.

[**Scully** *goes into the hall, where* **Tony** *mocks his forthcoming* *appearance on stage*]

Tony: Oh, Romeo, Romeo –

[**Scully** *goes out of the front door*]

8   The park

We see the park at dusk. **Scully** *creeps confidentially across the screen, followed instantly by* **Mooey.** *We hear them talk as they go.*

Scully: Nah, we had to have Mad Dog, Mooey. I know he's got rabies, but his mam's got a pram. Know what I mean.

Mooey: Er, yeah, it's got something to do with havin' a baby, hasn't it?

[*We then see* **Mad Dog** *coming into view following the other two. There is a pause, then* **Snotty Dog** *crosses with a pram and baby*]

9   The park

We see the park a few moments later. **Scully** *appears from the opposite direction, followed at a distance by* **Mad Dog** *with a pram full of saplings. We see* **Snotty Dog** *bringing up the rear, carrying a crying baby.*

10   A Residential Estate

We see a similar scene, except in a residential estate. **Scully's** *in the lead, followed closely by* **Mooey.** *There is a gap and then* **Mad Dog** *back into vision holding a single stunted sapling. He* *is pointing angrily at something out of vision. We then see the problem:* **Snotty Dog** *walking a pram with one howling baby inside.*

Mad Dog: Go home, will y'... I said go home... I'll kill y', I will, I'll kill y'...

[*We focus on* **Scully** *and* **Mooey**]

Scully: Only one tree left an' not even nine o'clock. Good hey, Moo?

Mooey: Yis!... But, er, do I really have to say all that about bein' an orphan?

Scully: Course y' do. Y' even had a feller cryin' in Sycamore Avenue.

Mooey: But, er, what do they want trees for, Scull?

Scully: They like trees around here.

Mooey: Oh. Er... why do some of them wink at us when they buy them?

Scully: 'Cos they buy them at seventy-five pence each an' they know where they come from at that price. They're just like us, most of them – 'cept they wear carpet slippers. They don't care neither.

[*The scene fades as we hear* **Mad Dog** *making* **Snotty Dog** *cry in the distance, and we also hear* **Snotty Dog**'s *injured and plaintive tone*]

Snotty Dog: You only wanted me for me pram...

11   Outside Steve's semi-detached house

We see the boys approaching the door.

Scully: We only want fifty pence f' this, Moo, it's the runt in the family.

[**Scully** *knocks on the door as he talks, and* **Mad Dog** *pushes* **Mooey** *forward, giving him the stunted sapling.* **Mooey** *holds the sapling like a lance, and mumbles his 'speech'*]

Mooey: It's hard in an orphanage, missus, y' hardly ever get t' see y' mam an' dad, especially if they're dead . . . it's hard bein' an orphan . . .

[*We see* **Snotty Dog** *whisper pathetically from the garden gate*]

Snotty Dog: I don't mind carryin' the tree as well, y' know boys . . .

Mad Dog: Is he still here?

[**Mad Dog** *turns furiously and takes a couple of paces down the path to threaten* **Snotty Dog,** *and the front door of the house opens. We see* **Steve,** *with cardigan and slippers and pipe*]

Mooey: It's hard in an orchard, er, orphanage, mister.

Steve: Well well well, what are you doing around here?

Mooey: [*Promptly*] Sellin' trees. For the orph . . . [**Scully** *elbows him*]

Scully: Er well, er, it's like this, Steve . . .

[*We see* **Mad Dog** *facing the other way, putting his collar up and his head down, starting to edge down the path.* **Steve** *watches him*]

Snotty Dog: [*Happily*] It's all right, Mad Dog, it's only our teacher.

Mad Dog: [*Manically*] I'll kill him, I will, so help me, I'll kill him . . .

Steve: Go on then, Scull.

[*He watches as* **Mad Dog** *slides away and* **Scully** *fidgets,* **Mooey** *smiles and* **Snotty Dog** *gets hit in the face*]

Scully: No I know what you're thinkin', Steve, but as it happens, we were comin' home from the Scouts and we just found this tree.

Mooey: [*Knowledgeably, as* **Scully** *points down the path*] In the park.

Scully: No, no –

Mooey: Scully was right, I didn't need me spade, one tug an' they came up.

Scully: Take no notice, Steve, it was lyin' there by the side of your gate.

Mooey: I'm a poor orphan, mister, I come from a cracked, er, broken home.

Scully: Not now, Moo. [*He smiles at* **Steve**]

Mooey: Don't you want me to cry neither?

Scully: Y' will do in a minute, don't you worry. Look Steve, there's a reasonable explanation for this –

Steve: I'm sure there is, but if I were you, I'd do what I'm going to do now.

Scully: [*Uncertainly*] What's that?

Mooey: He's going to wink at us, Scull. Certain. [*He leans forward to see*]

Steve: I'm going to go in my house, make a cup of coffee, and watch the end of the big film. Now why don't you see sense and do that?

Mooey: Yis! Thanks mister, I don't mind if I do, but I'd rather have a cup of tea if there's – [*He is halfway into* **Steve's** *hall.* **Scully** *drags him back and throws him down the path*] ... Er OK, I'll have coffee then ...

[*We just glimpse* **Mad Dog** *at the gate snatch* **Mooey** *sideways into the darkness*]

Steve: [*Laughing*] What's up with him?

Scully: You weren't at our school when he was there, were y'? [**Steve** *shakes his head*] Well, it's a long story.

Steve: But a simple one.

Scully: Yeah, er better go now, Steve, might take your advice about you know ... [*He starts to walk away*] I'm sorry about blowin' up in the gym. It was like, you're havin' a good time an' wallop – Dracula's there after y' blood.

Steve: It's all right, son, forgotten. OK?

Scully: [*He nods*] But y' won't forget about Blackburn Rovers will y'?

Steve: [*Coming down the path*] I won't, but now listen, don't you forget that all I said was that I might take you over there, if you improved and worked hard. [**Scully** *nods and then begins to walk away.* **Steve** *speaks as he goes*] ... And you know what you need above all else, don't you?

[**Scully** *turns back, and sees* **Dalglish** *standing there in* **Steve's** *place*]

Dalglish: Dedication!

[**Scully** *turns for a second to the camera and screws up his eyes. He turns back:* **Dalglish** *has gone again and he sees* **Steve** *instead*]

Scully: Wha'?

Steve: Dedication!

Scully: Oh yeah. Yeah. Right. Thanks Steve. [**Scully** *turns away, stops, and then goes back to* **Steve**]

Steve: Just one more thing, Fran ...

Scully: I know, I know, y' don't have to tell me, Mrs Heath wants me to be in the Pantomime. Jeez, I'll get home tonight an' it'll be on 'News at Ten'.

[*He goes down the path and looks for the others. They are peeping around the side of* **Steve's** *gate. He approaches them. He takes the small sapling off* **Mooey,** *and is about to drop it*]

Snotty Dog: I'll carry that for y' Scull, no problem. I like carryin' things.

Mad Dog: Creep . . . [*As* **Snotty Dog** *puts the sapling at the side of the baby*]

Scully: Right, that's it for tonight. [*He looks at* **Mooey**] Nine trees at seventy-five pence each. What's that, Moo?

Mooey: Er, it's, er . . . a lot of money, Scull.

Snotty Dog: Is there anything else y'd like me to do, boys?

Mad Dog: Yeah. *Go home!*

[**Scully, Mooey** and **Mad Dog** *turn and run off, leaving* **Snotty Dog**]

Snotty Dog: But I helped, I'm an accessory . . .

[*As we fade, we see him kick the pram and then walk after them*]

15 A road

It is now dark, but we see **Scully, Mooey** *and* **Mad Dog** *walking along a road.* **Mad Dog** *turns around as he walks, effectively walking backwards. He grins happily. We see the glare of car headlights catching them.* **Scully** *and* **Mooey** *stop immediately, and* **Mad Dog** *backs into them.*

Mad Dog: Got rid of him at –

[*We see a police car cross over the road and pull up in front of them.* **Two policemen** *get out of the car and face the boys. One of the policemen has a painfully scarred face, as if broken glass has made a serious point – there is a whole circle of scars in the centre of his face*]

Scully: Oh no. Look who it is – Isaiah!

[*They look –* **Mooey** *with interest*]

Scully: [*To the camera*] He's called Isaiah 'cos one eye's 'igher than the other.

Isaiah: All right plums, where's the trees?

Scully: Trees?

Isaiah: The trees out of the park, come 'head, Scully.

Scully: I dunno – they're still there, I suppose.

Mooey: [*Sagely*] Not all of them, Scull.

Isaiah: Oh aye, an' who're you when you're out?

Mooey: Er, the same person as I am when I'm in. I think.

Scully: Take no notice, boss, y' know. [*He motions his head, and whistles*]

Mooey: Would it be a good time to cry now, Scull?

Isaiah: Look, there's trees missin' from the park, accordin' the message I've got, and we've had angry ratepayers phonin' up about some kids walkin' around, tryin' to sell them trees. Now I know it's not a crime of international proportions, but it's the kind of soft trick a little no-mark like you'd get up to, and I'm very bored, so I might just get unpleasant. Understand?

Mooey: Er, no. You lost me when you got onto portions. I – [**Isaiah** *shoves him against a hedge, hard.* **Mooey** *looks at him*] Er, hey, I remember you now, but you didn't have the scars then. [**Scully** *winces*] Er, no, you caught me robbin' crab apples when I was little, an' you made me eat them all. Every single one. Yeah, I bent down the next day an' nearly shot the dog. [*He laughs loudly and gets shoved into the hedge*]

Isaiah: All right, I'm warnin' you. Tell me now.

Scully: There's nothin' to tell. We never did it. For a start, how could we walk around carryin' trees? What d' you think we are – lumberjacks? Y' need a spade, an axe an' a wheelbarrow f' a start . . .

Mooey: Or a pra – [**Isaiah** *knocks him down again*]

Isaiah: You stay out of this.

Scully: If y' wanna search us for the trees, y' welcome. You've probably noticed we're not hidin' wheelbarrows in obvious places.

[**Scully** *puts his hands up in the air sardonically. We see* **Mad Dog** *join him, and then we hear a baby crying in the distance. They glance back the way the came. We see* **Snotty Dog** *coming towards them with the pram and child, and tree. We see* **Snotty Dog** *hesitate as* **Isaiah** *starts talking again. He thinks about turning back and then crosses over the road*]

Isaiah: Okay, smartarse. [*He prods* **Scully** *in the chest*] No trees an' no nothing an' maybe it wasn't you this time, but I'm tellin' y', you, I've been after you for a long time – there's not a wall in this town that hasn't got your name on it.

Scully: That was years ago when I was a kid. I don't do that now. It's soft.

Isaiah: Why don't y' scrub it off then?

Scully: I hate community work.

Isaiah: That's because y' not part of the community. You don't belong where decent people are – y' the dregs, and

I'm going to make it my job t' bottle you up an' throw y' in the bin. Where y' belong.

Scully: Yeah, all right.

[*We focus on* **Snotty Dog,** *who is now getting closer*]

Isaiah: Don't forget. I'm goin' to have you. [*He too looks at* **Snotty Dog,** *who immediately, blindly, crosses the road*] Hey you – you with the pram.

Snotty Dog: [*Looking around for other people with prams*] Who, me?

Isaiah: [*As the police radio starts crackling out a message, and the other* **policeman** *goes towards the car*] Wha' time d' you call this, walkin' around with a baby?

Snotty Dog: [*At the kerb, going through his green cross code slowly*] It's me mam, mister. She's under two doctors.

Isaiah: There's no answer to that. Come on, hurry up.

[**Snotty Dog** *approaches him.* **Scully** *motions for the others to slide off. The other* **policeman** *leans out of the car.*

Second policeman: Frank, there's murder outside the Bluebell.

Isaiah: [*To* **Snotty Dog**] You, get home now. [*To the others*] And remember what I've said.

[*He gets back in the police car. It departs with a scream of tyres*]

Scully: [*To the camera*] Isaiah, our friendly community policeman. So friendly he's been tryin' to put me away for years – borstal trainin' f' droppin' litter, that's his plan of campaign.

[**Snotty Dog** *approaches, and lowers the hood of the pram, showing the small sapling stuck by the side of the unhappy baby*]

Snotty Dog: Good hey, boys, see how I kept me cool under pressure.

Mad Dog: Yeah great, an' f' that, y' know what y' can do? *Go home!*

Scully: [*As* **Snotty Dog** *gets near to tears*] Nah, come on, Snotty Dog, we'll count you in. [**Scully** *takes the sapling and this time throws it high into the air and into someone's garden. They begin walking away from us*] All right Moo, here's a good one for y', what's four into seventy five multiplied by nine . . . take your time.

Mooey: I'll need about three years for that. [*They all laugh*] . . . It's, er, well, er, four by, er . . . multiplied by, er . . . it's, er, . . . it's, er . . . not a lot of money, Scull.

[*They wander off down the road*]

Scully (Andrew Schofield) comes face to face with Leslie Brady (Sam Kelly)

Episode 3

Episode 3

1   A classroom

*We see a classroom, with a blackboard full of the family tree of the Habsburg dynasty, and the **teacher** at the desk, lifting his head up from his copy of* Punch *for a second and sniffing. We see the class, which consists of about fifteen boys, the dregs of the fifth year, including **Mad Dog** and **Brian Bignall**, all in the various stages of staring, terminal boredom. We come to **Scully** at a window near the back, with his desk up. He is eating a bag of chips and reading a football comic. He becomes aware of a dark shadow just behind him. He looks up and back, and sees the **teacher** looking down at him. **Scully** smiles and offers him a chip. The **teacher** points to the door. **Scully** gets up.*

2   The corridor outside the headmaster's room

*We see **Scully** as he comes out of the door marked 'Headmaster', wringing his hands. He walks down the corridor towards the hall. As he goes past the school hall, he glances in. He walks on a pace or two, then stops and goes back.*

3   The school hall and corridor

Scully *peeps into the hall furtively. We see **Mrs Heath** with* *some smaller children, giving them auditions for the pantomime, while* **Steve** *is up a ladder playing with lights.* **Scully** *looks away, and sees* **Joanna** *walking towards him and the hall doorway. He looks away as she walks into the hall. Then he looks at her as she goes in. She turns around and catches him, and she smiles at him. He half smiles, then stops and looks away. He looks away just in time to see a teacher,* **Leslie Brady***, hurtling towards him, carrying a virtual arsenal of visual aids and exercise books, plus several rolls of wallpaper, and losing control of the lot. He begins to run blindly with them as they escape his grasp. Whatever way* **Scully** *manages to move, he blindly moves that way too, till he cascades into* **Scully***. Books,* **Leslie** *and* **Scully** *are spreadeagled, with a bang and a clatter. The caretaker,* **Dracula,** *approaches, broom in hand, and helps to drag* **Scully** *out of the heap.* **Scully** *flinches, then looks puzzled as* **Dracula** *brushes him down and pats him on the head.* **Scully** *sees* **Mrs Heath** *and* **Joanna** *approaching from the hall. He begins to walk away. He looks behind himself, and still sees* **Dracula** *smiling at him, while* **Leslie** *struggles unassisted. He see* **Mrs Heath** *at the doorway, and turns away quickly. He glances darkly at us.*

4   The classroom

We see **Scully** *back in the lesson. Nothing has changed, except that his chips have gone, and the* **teacher** *is now smoking the chalk as well as reading* Punch*. We see the class and the* **teacher** *as* **Scully** *talks to us flatly, without anger.*

Scully: It is though, it's last at school. There's nothin' down for y'. Not for our class anyway. Some of us in here give up tryin' at playschool. But it's all right, 'cos most of the teachers gave up before we were born. [*As he talks to us, we see* **Joey Kelly** *begin to flick soggy paper at* **Scully**, *who* *mainly ignores him, apart from the odd glare*] But the worst part is that at least in gaol you can get time off for good behaviour but in school if you creep to the teachers, they give you another couple of years and stick you in the sixth form. [**Kelly** *flicks a pen and it hits* **Scully** *who, without looking, frisbees his history book at* **Kelly**. *He keeps talking*] No thanks, y' not goin' to catch me stayin' on – y' may as well go on the dole straight away around here than after you've been to university.

[**Kelly** *throws his kit bag straight at* **Scully** *who hurtles it back at him.* **Kelly** *howls loudly, but the* **teacher** *has already seen* **Scully** *throw the kit bag*]

Teacher: [*A command*] Headmaster!

Scully: Er no, he's somewhat taller than me, Sir, and his operation's left him with a permanent –

Teacher: Get out! Go on, get out now! I will not have physical violence!

Scully: [*He mumbles as he goes*] Y' wanna tell the headmaster that . . .

5   The corridor outside the headmaster's office

We hear a door slam. We are outside the headmaster's office. **Scully** *leans back against the door, holding his backside. He sees* **Steve** *and* **Mrs Heath** *facing him, waiting.*

Scully: [*Turning as if to go back in*] I'd rather have another two on the backside.

Steve: Than what?

Scully: You know. Everyone knows. Once you two start walkin' around like the Dynamic Duo, it can only mean one thing – pantomime time. But not for me. It's bad enough bein' here as it is.

Mrs Heath: And whose fault is that?

Scully: [*Genuinely angry*] Wha'? *What?* Whose fault d' y' think it is – 'cos it's not mine, love. I'll tell y' what school's for, for most of us – it's so y' can get used to what happens to y' when y' leave school. [*He stops and waits, but doesn't tempt either of them into asking*] An' y' know what happens to y' then – *nothin'.*

Mrs Heath: [*Standing back critically*] Very good . . . Now I'm casting the leading parts after school this afternoon. I'll come down to your classroom and get you, Francis, if you don't mind.

[*She turns and sweeps away.* **Steve** *stays a second or so and grins at* **Scully,** *who stares helplessly at him.* **Steve** *goes*]

Scully: Talk to yourself, Scully, y' may as well, 'cos nobody listens to y' anyway.

[**Scully** *goes to walk away, and* **Dracula** *steps out of a doorway, as if waiting for him. He approaches* **Scully,** *brushing the floor as he comes.* **Scully** *doesn't have the energy to escape. He looks around – at his side of the wall we see a crucifix.* **Scully** *glances at the camera, then looks towards* **Dracula**

We see a quick insert of **Dracula** *as 'Dracula', dripping blood and approaching. We see* **Scully** *grab the crucifix off the wall. He holds it in front of himself and shields his eyes.*

We cut back to **Dracula** *dressed in dungarees, looking surprised. We see that* **Scully** *has actually got the crucifix in his hand.* **Scully** *looks at the crucifix, touches its corners and puts it back*]

Scully: I, er, made it in woodwork, y' see, just lookin' how it was goin' on . . .

Dracula: Very good.

Scully: [*Suspiciously*] Yeah . . .

Dracula: [*Not looking*] About the other night, Scully, the bike, and the gymnasium. When I . . . when I . . .

Scully: Threw a wobbler?

Dracula: When I was upset. I just thought, you know, let bygones be bygones – I mean, it might not have been you who . . . who . . . p-pa- did that to my bike. So, er, forgive an' forget eh?

Scully: Er, yeah . . . if you say so. [**Scully** *starts to slide away*]

Dracula: Good, good . . . I hear you want to be a footballer? [**Scully** *stops*]

Scully: So?

Dracula: Oh nothing – your mother was telling me the other night, that was all . . . it's a funny thing, I didn't know who your mother was, till the other . . . I never knew Mrs Barrett's friend was your mother. Funny that, isn't it? All that time and I only knew her as . . . Mrs Barrett's friend . . . [*Winks at* **Scully**] Mrs Barrett and I were good friends. We had things in common.

Scully: Yeah, I heard she was a blood donor.

Dracula: [*A glint of fang*] Are you being smart?

Scully: I hope so. An' seein' as you were sayin' about forgive an' forget . . .

Dracula: Yes?

Scully: It was me who painted Dracula on y' bike.

[**Scully** *races bowlegged away. He turns at the end of the corridor and sees* **Dracula** *dressed as 'Dracula'. As a* **small boy** *passes we see* **Dracula** *slamming his fangs into the boy and dragging him onto the floor in a flurry, just as the boy* *reaches for the crucifix on the wall. The bell goes for the end of morning school]*

6   Outside a sports shop

First we see a huge picture of Kenny Dalglish, six by six. The camera pulls away to show that it is in a sports shop window. We see **Scully** *leaning against the window, talking to the picture, as he finishes off a portion of chips.*

Scully: Am I seein' you or what? [*He looks around, then turns back to the picture and throws the chip paper away*]

Scully: I mean . . . look, when I see you, are you there? 'Cos it seems as if you are . . . as if I can really see you . . . when I see you. If you . . . see what I mean. [*We see the reflection of* **Joanna** *in the window, watching* **Scully**. *He doesn't see it*] The thing is, I don't normally see things when they're not there . . . except when I want to see them. It's – [*He sees* **Joanna's** *reflection, and stays still*]

Joanna: You can get put away for talking to yourself. [*She smiles and sweeps into the sports shop. He speaks to her and follows her in*]

Scully: No, er, I was . . . Hiya, it's, er, Joanna, isn't it? [*She nods*] I was . . . just thinking out loud, you know, thoughts . . . like. Are you going back to school?

Joanna: Are you?

Scully: I, er, wasn't going to, but I am now.

Joanna: I've got to go home first though.

Scully: S' all right, it's on the way.

[**Scully** *goes to turn away, delighted.* **Mooey** *enters, and they try to leave*]

Mooey: Er, all right, Scull! Great! [*He looks at* **Scully's** *hostility*] Er, I'm celebratin', Scull, but er . . . I've got no one to celebrate with. [*As they go out*] I've had a smart mornin' y'know, y'wanna know what's happened to me this mornin'?

Scully: Not really.

7 A road

We see them as they walk away. **Mooey's** *first move is to get in the middle, by force if necessary. He keeps trying to unscrew a bottle of lemonade without giving away the other bottle – he has lost too many possessions in this manner. Consequently, he never gets to drink a drop.*

Mooey: No, it's the best thing that's ever happened to me in me whole life, the very best! This is like . . . like . . . when me mam took me to Butlins. Only better. 'Cos when we went to Butlins I fell off the Big Dipper on the first day an' er, spent all week in Minehead General Hospital, an' ever since then I've had these . . .

Scully: Yeah all right, go on.

Mooey: What?

Scully: The best day of y' life! [**Joanna** *grins*]

Mooey: Good job y' reminded me, Scull. Y'know what happened to me this mornin'. [**Scully** *and* **Joanna** *exchange glances across* **Mooey**] It was like . . . like when me Mam took me to Butl . . .

Joanna: What was it Mooey?

Mooey: Our metalwork teacher made me . . . the captain of the football team! Yis! Double yis! Captain!

Scully: The metalwork teacher?

Mooey: Yea, he takes us for football as well.

Scully: Figures.

Mooey: But captain.

Scully: Very good that Moo. [*Stops*] Tell y' what, why don't y' nip back to that sports shop an' have a look at some football boots, hey? Y' gonna need them now, Captain, an' we'll . . .

Mooey: Oh no, we don't play any matches . . .

8 Outside Mooey's house

The three continue their walk.

Mooey: I was so happy, Scull, I was over the parrot . . . they say that, footballers, y'know, I was over the parrot . . .

Scully: I'm the opposite, Moo, I'm as sick as a moon . . .

Joanna: What else did you do this morning?

Mooey: We, er, had games this morning. [*He nods*] All mornin'.

Scully: All mornin'? *All mornin'*?

[*They are now outside* **Joanna's** *house*]

Mooey: Er, yeah. Apart from beef curry, spotted dick an' prayers.

Joanna: [*Smiling*] Can anyone go to your school?

Mooey: I dunno. I'll have to ask the coach driver.

Joanna: Who?

Mooey: The coach driver. When he picks us up in the mornin' he won't let anyone else on. But y' can ask him if y' want. He let Albie Brown's mam on last week. [*He smiles gently at them*] Captain . . . yis.

Scully and Joanna: Right –

Scully: I'll er – [*Pointing at* **Joanna's** *house*] wait for y'.

[*She smiles at him.* **Mooey** *comes between them, effortlessly*]

Mooey: I knew somethin' was up, y' know, Scull, when he took me in his little room where he keeps his chisels. [**Scully** *is trying to watch* **Joanna** *walking towards her door*] I was lookin' for his baseball bat, 'cos that's what he hits y' with when he's angry, but –

[**Scully** *grabs* **Mooey** *and hauls him away from* **Joanna's** *path towards the privets by* **Mooey's** *house, where* **Joanna** *cannot see his imminent brutality*]

Scully: See that, Moo? [*He shows* **Mooey** *his left fist.* **Mooey** *examines it, looks up at* **Scully,** *and nods*] Well, that's not the one that's goin' to hit y'.

[*He slaps* **Mooey** *across the head with his right hand. It doesn't hurt, but is not exactly loving. We hear and then see* **Marie Morgan** *lounging at the Morgans' doorway*]

Marie: Oh my God, Francis, you're so tough and . . . butch these days, just like Charles Bronson. Mmm! Do it again, I like it . . .

[*She approaches their gate, and* **Scully** *looks sideways towards* **Joanna's** *gate. In the distance, some girls of the same age are approaching.* **Marie** *pouts across the gate*]

Marie: I'm free about nine, if you want to slap me about a little . . .

Mooey: Y'd better go, Scull, y' not safe when Marie starts talkin' like that, even our dog hides.

Marie: Get in there an' make some toast.

Mooey: Er, we haven't got any bread.

Marie: Use y' imagination. Get in. Now! [*She opens the gate savagely.* **Mooey** *winces away to the door*] Well Francis –

Mooey: I haven't got any imagination, Marie, they taught us that in school, an' they told me I haven't got any . . .

[**Marie** *lacerates him from ten yards. He admits defeat and goes*]

Marie: So where are we going, Francis? When shall we meet?

[*The girls giggle past, then turn and look at* **Scully** *and* **Marie**. **Scully** *glares at them, and moves slightly away from* **Marie**. *The girls are approaching* **Joanna's** *gate. Inevitably,* **Joanna** *reaches the gate at the same time.* **Scully** *watches.* **Marie** *watches* **Scully**. **Mooey** *refuses to admit defeat, and sneaks towards* **Marie** *and* **Scully**.

We see **Joanna** *look towards* **Scully**, *smile and shrug slightly. She turns and walks away with the other girls. Once, she turns back.* **Scully** *closes his eyes and turns back towards* **Marie** *and* **Mooey**. **Mooey** *is holding his nose.* **Marie** *smiles sweetly*]

Marie: I'm not going back to school . . .

Scully: Neither am I!

[*He turns and walks the opposite way.* **Mooey** *crashes through the privets after him*]

9 Outside Scully's house

It is a few minutes later. We see **Scully** *followed, a yard or two behind, by* **Mooey**. *As* **Scully** *reaches his house, he looks for his key, then knocks on the door. The door is opened by* **Arthur**, *wearing a girl's school uniform with no affectation nor snigger. It fits him well, and he is unconcerned.*

Scully: Sorry, wrong house. [*Misses a beat*] Where did you get that?

Arthur: Me an' Janice Cook swopped. But she let me keep me conkers.

[**Arthur** *goes into the house.* **Mooey** *has been staring at* **Arthur**]

Mooey: There's something different about that sister of yours, you know.

[*As* **Scully** *is about to go into the house, we hear his* **Gran** *singing 'Once I had a Secret Love', being carried by* **two very elderly well-dressed gents.** *She is legless*]

Gran: Hang on, Francis . . .

[*We see the* **two old gents** *remove* **Gran's** *arm from around them. They prop her up.* **Scully** *and* **Mooey** *put their arms around her, and begin to take her in*]

Scully: Array Gran. It's only ten past one . . .

Gran: Don't go away, fellers, I won't be long . . .

10   Scully's hall

Scully, Mooey *and* **Gran** *get inside and close the door on the* **two elderly gents.**

Gran: I can't stand neither of them, if the truth be told, but someone's got to take me out . . . [*They move her towards the living room*] I like the barman out of the 'Bluebell' the best, but I've told him straight, I won't be the cause of a broken marriage . . .

11   Scully's living room

We see the living room as **Scully** *and* **Mooey** *bring* **Gran** *in.* **Mrs Barrett** *and* **Tony** *are sitting on the couch near the TV.*

Arthur *is on the floor, feet up in the air, reading* Woman. **Henry** *is sitting on the floor in the corner, listening to train sounds, while* **Rita**, **Tony's** *girlfriend, is in an armchair, looking furious and very overweight.* **Tony** *is making* **Mrs Barrett** *laugh warmly. He digs her in the ribs.* **Scully** *and* **Mooey** *plop* **Gran** *onto a vacant chair. 'News at One' is on television.*

Gran: Oh God, those Pina Coladas . . . I'll be all right in a minute, when the pineapples go down . . .

[**Scully** *sits on the arm of the chair and* **Mooey** *stands at his side, very happy. Everything here is so normal for him*]

Scully: Dracula was askin' after you today, Mrs Barrett.

Mrs Barrett: [*Giggling*] And who in God's name is Dracula?

Tony: Oh he's a bit of a fly-by-night. A fly-by-night! Dracula!

Rita: [*Suddenly*] Tell your brother he's stupid.

Scully: Henry, you're stupid.

[**Henry** *looks up with disinterest*]

Tony: She means me. Tell her it's mutual.

Scully: Tell her yourself.

Mooey: Er, I'll tell her if y' want.

Gran: [*Just as suddenly, out of her sleep*] I don't feel well!

Scully: [*With no malice*] You never do, Gran.

Gran: I know, it's because I'm old. I hate bein' old. [*She snores*]

Rita: I'm goin'. [*Pause*] I said I'm goin'.

Mooey: Tara. Been nice meetin' y'. I'm the captain of the football team.

Rita: Tony, I'm goin'. I won't say it again. [*Pause*] I'm goin'.

Tony: Yeah, all right.

[**Rita** *stands up and storms out. We hear doors banging.* **Mooey** *slides into* **Rita's** *seat quietly*]

Mrs Barrett: You're awful, you are, Tony.

Tony: Ah, she'll be all right, she'll soon forget.

Scully: I thought elephants never forgot.

[**Tony** *points a finger at him as we hear the front door opening*]

Mrs Scully: [*At the door*] I won't tell you two again! Go on, beat it!

[**Tony** *nearly jumps off the couch, and away from* **Mrs Barrett**. **Arthur** *tries to get between the couch and the wall.* **Scully** *groans*]

Tony: Me mam, me mam! What's she doin' home? I'm ill, all right? I'm ill. [*He drapes himself on the couch, holding his head*]

Mrs Scully: Bloody Dad's Army . . . Mam! [*She enters, sees her mother, and is dismayed. She sees the others, also to her dismay*] What are you lot doin' here? And you, Arthur, get those clothes off, I've had just murder with Janice Cook's mother. When was the last time you changed your socks? [**Arthur** *sneaks off*] [*To* **Tony**] Well come on. [**Tony** *groans*] What're y' doin' home?

Tony: [*An imitation of Brando dying in* Mutiny on the Bounty] Hypertension, Mam. I've been takin' me work too serious, the Boss said.

Mrs Scully: You won't be much longer, the way y' shapin' up.

Tony: Anyway, mam, what about you?

Mrs Scully: Short time. [**Tony** *laughs, and is met by looks of anger from* **Scully** *and* **Mrs Scully**] Talkin' of short time, you owe me ten pounds. Where were you last night?

Tony: I was out, Mam. With er, Rita.

Mrs Scully: All night?

Scully: They went to the 'Elephant and Castle'. Well, it was only called the 'Castle' till Rita went there.

Tony: You've had it, you. [*He stands up to get his money out, shakily. He almost faints as he gets the money out*] Me an' Rita won't be able to go out tonight now, Mam. You know.

Mrs Scully: I wouldn't worry. I've just seen her, she said to poison y' dinner. [*To* **Scully**] If y' not in school in five minutes y' goin' to be in trouble.

Scully: It's OK, Mam. [*Looking around the room*] I think I'd rather be in school than a madhouse.[*He goes towards the door*]

Mooey: Er, I wouldn't, er, there's a big film on in a minute, y' know . . .

[**Mooey** *looks around beguilingly, and moves the chair nearer to the television.* **Scully** *and* **Mrs Scully** *exchange grins.* **Scully** *goes*]

12   The classroom

Scully *is back in class. There is no teacher, and the class are dead-eyed again, except for* **Joey Kelly** *who is carving 'Scully is a dead man' on a desk that is already scarred with 'Kelly is cool/sexy/smart/ace/king/rules'.* **Scully** *(like a few others) has his feet up on the desk.*

Scully: [*To the camera*] We're waitin' for a teacher. It could be a long wait. It's gettin' that bad, even the teachers are waggin' off now. Mind you, if you do get a good teacher for a lesson in our school, you lock the door and keep him in after the bell goes, 'cos y' can be guaranteed that the next one through the door must be a disaster area.

[*The door opens right on cue. Amid the sniggers of expectation we see* **Leslie Brady,** *a sad middle-aged man. He wears a permanently shell-shocked, startled look, and carries a briefcase, visual aids and rolls of wallpaper under his arm. He is benign and nervous; a dreadful victim*]

Scully: [*To the camera*] See what I mean.

Leslie: Good afternoon, Five S. I've er, never had you before ... have ... have I? [*There are sniggers from the class*] My name's Leslie erm – [*Laughter*] Yes, Leslie Brady. Now ... see if you would, erm ... I'm, er, I've – I'm a replacement for your ... erm, Mrs, er, she's ill ... I normally take the younger classes but ... this is Maths. [*More laughter*] I'm ... I've come to teach you the Pythagoras Theory.

[*He is about to throw the wallpaper that is attached to two pieces of wood over the blackboard, but turns as* **Kelly** *speaks*]

Kelly: The wha?

[**Leslie** *turns as he throws – and misses. The wallpaper spills onto the floor. He speaks as he turns and scrambles for the paper*]

Leslie: It's a ... it's a sort of puzzle.

Kelly: I know – so are you.

[*Cheap laughter, mainly from* **Kelly**]

Leslie: No I'm not. And it's, erm, a mathematical puzzle. I think you'll enjoy it, it's, er . . . enjoyable. Really.

[*He turns again.* **Scully** *looks at the camera, and speaks quietly to us*]

Scully: Y' wanna go now. No y' do. Honest. This isn't goin' to be very nice . . . Suit yourself. But I'm havin' nothin' to do with it – I've been battered enough already today.

[**Leslie** *has rolled up his wallpaper and now begins to throw the roll over the blackboard. He pulls the wallpaper down, one side facing – the side without the pretty bedroom patterns of roses. We see 'The Principles of Pythagoras'. As he does this, his back turned, the class, silently, and apart from* **Scully** *and* **Bignall,** *begin to throw things at him. There is no obvious organization, but it starts with* **Kelly** *throwing soggy balls of paper. Soon, as* **Leslie** *stands there, very still, pens, pencils, books, bags, ashtrays made in metalwork, old comics and bits of plaster off the wall come flying in his direction. As soon as he turns around, everyone stops immediately, and sits still with their arms folded, staring at him. We can see* **Leslie** *pluck up his courage to speak to them*]

Leslie: Now that was silly, wasn't it? [*The class nods in agreement, except* **Kelly** *who shakes his head*] Was there any point in your behaviour? [*The whole class shakes its head, except* **Kelly,** *who nods*] [*Happily*] Right, good, fine, that's sorted out, thank you. Now would the . . . erm, culprits please come out and pick it all up?

[*We see* **Joey Kelly** *saunter out and pick up the smallest piece of soggy paper he can find. He smiles sweetly at* **Leslie** *and walks back. Others join him. There are still some items on the floor – the articles that could have maimed.* **Leslie** *grins, and turns back to the board. Immediately most of the*

*class let him have it again, and he turns around just in time
to see* **Kelly** *throw half a desk lid.* **Leslie** *lets it hit him on the
shoulder although he could have avoided it. There is
absolute silence.* **Leslie** *rubs his shoulder and talks in a
whisper, but still twitching nervously]*

Leslie: Come here.

[**Kelly** *approaches slowly, trying to look humble and clean-
living]*

Leslie: Why did you do that?

Kelly: I don't know, sir, I don't know what came over me . . .
I think it was all the others doin' it sir.

[**Leslie** *puts both his hands on* **Kelly's** *shoulders as he
talks.* **Kelly** *stays still but looks from one hand to the other
wildly]*

Leslie: Are you sorry?

Kelly: Yes sir.

Leslie: Truly sorry?

Kelly: Oh yes, sir, truly very sorry sir.

Leslie: What's your name, child?

Kelly: Don't send me for the cane, sir, I've got weak
hands.

Leslie: I just want to know your name, that's all.

Kelly: Leroy, sir. Leroy Constantine.

Leslie: How interesting. Did you know that was a West
Indian name?

Kelly: Yes sir, my father was a sailor, sir.

Leslie: Well – [*He stops and looks at* **Kelly** *who looks the
model of innocence*] – well, Leroy, let's stop being childish,
shall we? Pick it up. Pick it up and put it back with the rest
of the desk.

Kelly: Yes sir, thank you sir. God bless you sir. [**Kelly** *picks up the half lid and walks back, grinning hugely*]

Leslie: [*Smiling*] Come out and get your weapons. Any left over, I keep.

[*As they drift out to gather their weapons,* **Bignall** *slides over and sits by* **Scully**. **Bignall** *is a big lad but appears to be stoic*]

Bignall: This is daft.

Scully: I know. He shouldn't be here – he should be somewhere quiet takin' tablets. [*They glance up and smile.* **Bignall** *glances at his watch before resting his head on the desk*]

Bignall: Half three. Another twenty-five minutes.

Scully: Yeah, an' then Mrs Heath. [**Bignall** *looks at him.* **Scully** *shakes his head*] Trainin' tonight?

Bignall: [*Nods*] Fight on Monday. Final eliminators. [*Grinning*] Gonna kill him.

[**Kelly** *has come around behind* **Scully** *and* **Bignall** *as they talk. He has a piece of paper and a felt-tip pen in his hand*]

Kelly: Good hey, hey – see me then – Leroy Constantine. I didn't half hit him as well, didn't I? I bet he's hurt, y' know. I wouldn't be surprised if I broke somethin'.

Scully: Kelly. [**Kelly** *looks at him*] You're stupid.

Kelly: You're dead after. Me an' my gang 're goin' to see to that. We'll be waitin' for you. Wherever you go, we'll be –

Bignall: [*With his head down*] Shut up, Kelly.

Kelly: Yeah, all right, sorry Brian. [*He goes back to his paper, and starts writing*] Er, how d'you spell 'breasts'?

[**Scully** and **Bignall** *look at each other wryly. They glance up, and see* **Leslie** *with his hands up, facing the class and now sitting*]

Leslie: OK boys, one free shot.

[*We see the class looking at each other. Nothing is thrown*]

Scully: [*Flatly*] He thinks he's a coconut.

[*Laughter*]

Leslie: Fine good, a little humour to lighten the proceedings. [*He laughs*] Now seriously, who knows anything about the Pythagoras Theory?

[*We see a lot of blank faces as we fade . . .*

We come back, some time later, as **Leslie** *is completing his discussion on the Pythagoras Theorem. He glances at his watch*]

Leslie: Erm, yes, so er that's the er, Pythagoras Theorem. In a nutshell. As it were. Now if you would get your notebooks out and . . . copy my explanation off the wallpa – board, as it is. [*Nobody moves*] No? Oh. [*He looks at his watch again*] Erm, I'll just . . . [*He motions towards the wallpaper*] . . . and then we'll . . . [*Waves his hands*] . . . we'll do something else. Yes?

[*He turns towards the wallpaper, flinches for a second, then begins to take it down and laboriously fold it up, his back turned. As he does so,* **Mad Dog** *and the boy sitting next to him quietly move their desk forward towards him. They turn and grin, and other boys start moving their desks. A noise is finally made.* **Leslie** *turns around, and everyone stays very still.* **Leslie** *knows something is happening, but doesn't quite know what it is. He turns away, and the class lift and move again, like a corporate beast – all except for* **Scully** *and*

Bignall *who are now reading comics, and* **Kelly** *who is busy composing his story with pictures.*

Leslie *turns around as the boys have blocked off the doorway with their desks. They sit facing him like a matured village of the damned.* **Leslie** *looks away, and then looks back quickly. He just sees them as they compose themselves, a foot or so nearer. The space between the doorway and the teacher's desk is eroding fast.* **Leslie** *turns and goes to the desk: the space is filled. When he sits down, he is surrounded. He tries to compose himself. He folds his arms, unfolds them, and strangles his hands*]

Leslie: Are we sitting comfortably? Then I ... I shall begin.

[*He grins, and looks at the boys close to him. A paper plane loops towards him and hits him on the forehead, dropping on to his desk amongst ribald cheering.* **Leslie** *looks down at the plane, and then looks up. It could only have come from* **Bignall**, **Scully** *or* **Kelly** *– except that* **Kelly** *has moved as he threw it and is now in the centre of the room, sitting alone and angelic.* **Leslie** *looks at* **Scully** *and* **Bignall**, *who look at him. He glances at* **Kelly**, *who motions with his finger behind his other hand at* **Scully** *and* **Bignall**. **Leslie** *picks up the paper plane and opens it, and becomes aghast and angry. He waves the paper about violently*]

Leslie: High spirits, yes – but – but – but filth – *no*! Who wrote this filth? Who? It came from over there!

[*As* **Leslie** *waves it about, we see the lads nearest trying to read it, and* **Leslie** *points towards* **Bignall** *and* **Scully**, *who look blankly at him and look down at their comics*]

Leslie: You two! [*A hand sneaks onto his desk to try to grab the plane: he smacks the hand almost without looking*] You two! Come here to me! [*They look at him again*] I said *here*!

[**Scully** and **Bignall** *finally stand up and climb between the desks. They finish up in the small space in front of* **Leslie**, *between his desk and the rest of the desks, ignoring whispers from the class, particularly* **Mad Dog**. *They look at* **Leslie** *with ill-concealed contempt.* **Bignall** *is nearest to* **Leslie**]

Leslie: [*To* **Bignall**] Was it you, boy? [*No answer*] Answer me! [**Bignall** *shakes his head sadly*] I said answer me!

[*He hits* **Bignall** *over the top of his head. To everyone's amazement, especially* **Leslie's**. *He grabs hold of the hand that hit* **Bignall** *with his free hand. There is absolute silence.* **Scully** *glances sidelong at the camera and winces. He puts his hand part-way over his eyes*]

Bignall: What?

Leslie: Was it you who threw the paper plane?

Bignall: No.

Leslie: No what?

Bignall: No it wasn't me what threw the paper plane.

Leslie: [*Near to tears, he hits* **Bignall** *again. The class stare, amazed*] I can't take much more.

Bignall: What was that for?

Leslie: Because of this! [*He waves the plane around again*] Filth, boy!

Bignall: I never did that, an' neither did he. [*Indicating* **Scully**]

Leslie: Of course you did. One of you must have. It came from where you were sitting. What else am I to think?

Bignall: [*Quietly spitting the words out*] I dunno. I dunno what you think, but I know what I think. I think you're cracked and you shouldn't be here, and what's more, I never wrote this or drew it or threw it. [*He flicks at the paper*] I'm good at biology. I know for a fact, girls don't have hair there.

[*There is some small laughter, but it stops as* **Leslie** *picks up his wallpaper hanger and starts battering* **Bignall** *with it. There is screaming and crying. They stumble together for a few seconds as the class stands on their chairs and the likes of* **Mad Dog** *look for blood.* **Leslie** *keeps trying to hit* **Bignall***, until* **Bignall** *hits him with a one–two, a left to the stomach, and as* **Leslie's** *head goes down, an uppercut, some of the class start counting 'one, two, three, four . . .' Then the bell goes, and they stop. There is silence as* **Leslie** *stands up. He looks at the mob between him and the door, blocking him in, and rapidly gathers together his equipment, twitching desperately*]

Leslie: I'm . . . very sorry. You . . . you won't be having me again. [*He smiles, opens the window by his desk, and throws his things out*] Good afternoon, Five . . . erm, Five S.

[*He climbs out of the window and walks away from school. The others stand on their desks and look at him, therefore hiding* **Scully** *from the door and the corridor.* **Bignall** *turns away*]

Bignall: Kelly, come here.

Kelly: [*Out of vision*] Er no, Brian, er y' see, I didn't . . . [*As* **Bignall** *goes towards* **Kelly***,* **Scully** *sees* **Mrs Heath** *coming down the corridor.* **Scully** *looks around quickly for an escape as* **Mrs Heath** *enters*]

Mrs Heath: Scully . . . Scully . . . excuse me . . . [*We hear* **Mrs Heath** *and* **Bignall** *as* **Scully** *moves across to the window*] Bignall what *are* you doing?

Bignall: It's only Kelly, Miss. [*We hear* **Kelly** *howl*]

Mrs Heath: Oh that's all right, carry on then . . . Scully . . . I know you're there . . .

[*We see* **Scully** *depart the same way as* **Leslie***, with* **Mrs Heath** *still struggling through the circle of desks*]

13 Outside the school

Scully *walks a few yards, turns and grins. He looks up and sees* **Steve** *at the classroom window above, pipe in mouth, watching* **Scully***. He shakes his head.* **Scully** *stops and looks to the bottom window. He sees* **Mrs Heath** *bravely trying to climb out. He then looks back up at* **Steve***, and sees* **Dalglish** *in the window, he too shaking his head at* **Scully***.*

Scully *sees* **Mrs Heath** *walking towards him and glances manically back at the window: he sees* **Steve** *only.* **Scully** *turns and runs off. As he runs further and further, he goes past the forlorn* **Leslie***, tramping away from the school, muttering to himself as he goes.*

Leslie: Ah good afternoon, headmaster, I'd just like to say goodbye . . . headmaster, you have a problem, yes, you've just . . . [*Giggling*] you've just lost a member of staff . . . yes, er no . . .

[**Scully** *runs past him and away as* **Leslie** *keeps walking*]

Episode 4

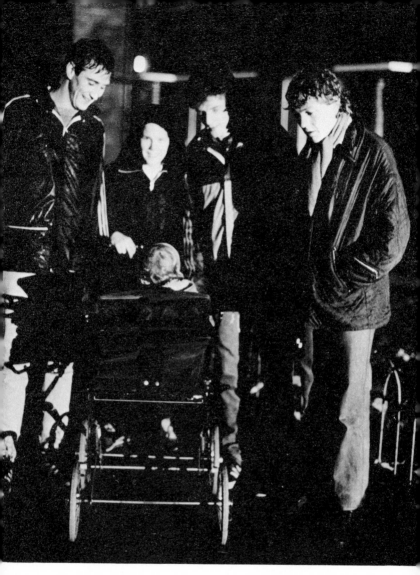

Mad Dog (Mark McGann), Snotty Dog (Richard Burke), Scully and Mooey surround Puppy Dog (Lucinda Scrivener) on a bad Friday night

Episode 4

1 Outside a public house

It is early evening. We see **Scully, Mooey** *and* **Mad Dog**
*standing on the steps of one of the area's rougher, larger public
houses. At the bottom of the steps stand* **Snotty Dog,** *baby and
pram.* **Mad Dog** *looks bored and angry.* **Scully** *finally glances
at the camera and speaks.*

Scully: Friday night. The big night out. No expense spared.
Know what I mean? [*He looks around at his surroundings,
half grins, and looks back at the camera*] This is where it all
happens.

[*Pause*]

Mad Dog: What're we gonna do now? [*Another pause*] Ah
come on, don't leave it up to me all the time.

[**Scully** *smiles wryly to himself*]

Snotty Dog: [*Hopefully, edging nearer*] I know, we
could –

Mad Dog: Shut it you. I'm fed up with you followin' me
around.

Snotty Dog: But Mad Dog –

Mad Dog: [*Furious*] An' me name's not Mad Dog, it's
Graham.

Scully: Why didn't y' bring a ball, Mad Dog?

Mad Dog: I er, sort of . . . I mean, it is *Friday night*. You're supposed to have a good time of a Friday night. Like . . . like Friday night's when you have a . . . [*Limply*] good time. I mean what are we going to do?

Scully: How much have we got Moo?

[*They all get money out*]

Mooey: Er, two ones, a little silver one, and a half.

[*They look at him blankly*]

Scully: You tell me Snotty Dog, what do you wanna do?

Snotty Dog: Er . . . er . . . er . . . we could set fire to the grass.

Scully: It's November, there is no grass, An' anyway, what happened to y' the last time y' did that?

Snotty Dog: Well . . .

Scully: Y' burnt y' hand, singed y' hair and melted the soles of y' best shoes.

[**Snotty Dog** *sniggers:* **Mad Dog** *hits him automatically*]

Snotty Dog: All right, we won't do that then. [*Silence*] This is no life y' know. [*More silence*] What are we gonna do now?

[**Scully** *looks out, and sees a police car sliding up.*

We see **Isaiah** *pull the window of the car down. He half leans out, 'smiles', and just points his finger away from the pub steps. They begin to move sourly away*]

Isaiah: And you, Scully, if I were you, on y' way home tonight I'd look for a fatal accident. Put us all out of our misery. [*He grins viciously at them, pulls the window back up, and indicates the driver to move on. They slide away into the night*]

Scully: It's difficult sometimes bein' famous.

[*They move away from us*]

Mooey: I know. Now I'm captain of the football team, everyone in school keeps askin' me for me autograph . . .

Mad Dog: [*To* **Snotty Dog**] Will you stop followin' me! And wipe y' nose f' God's sake.

Scully: Well, there's another good shirt sleeve ruined . . .

2   A shelter in the park

We see them in the shelter, staring out at the rain. **Snotty Dog** *and the pram are in the rain.*

Mad Dog: We could go an' sit in the launderette.

Scully: Ohhhh, dead excitin'. Y' makin' me tremble already.

Mad Dog: All right clever dick, *you* do better then.

[**Scully** *glances at us, rolls his shoulders, as if accepting the challenge, and strolls out of the shelter, pulling his collar up*]

3   A launderette

We see them in close-up on a bench seat, staring. Only **Mad Dog** *seems satisfied with life.* **Mooey's** *head is going around and around. The camera moves back to reveal that they are in the launderette.*

Mad Dog: Well at least we got in here.

Scully: Anyone can get in a launderette, Mad Dog. It's only one step above a police station f' gettin' in free an' havin' fun.

[*He walks away and* **Mooey** *looks at him; so does* **Snotty Dog**]

Mooey: Er, where y' goin' Scull, can I come?

Mad Dog: [*As* **Mooey** *follows* **Sculley**] Ahhh, I'm stayin' here.

[**Mad Dog** *folds his arms and pretends to be at ease.* **Snotty Dog** *watches* **Mooey** *and* **Scully** *walking away. He goes to follow them, but* **Mad Dog** *drags him back. There is a pause. As we focus on* **Mad Dog** *and* **Snotty Dog**, *we hear the door close.* **Mad Dog** *glances after* **Scully** *and* **Mooey**, *and squirms with indecision. He decides to follow them, and* **Snotty Dog** *naturally goes to follow* **Mad Dog**, *who turns and pushes him back down*]

Mad Dog: Will you stop followin' me – y' gettin' on me nerves.

[**Snotty Dog** *looks after* **Mad Dog** *as he exits, then turns to the pram and speaks into it quietly, with feeling*]

Snotty Dog: I hate you, Jason, I really hate you.

4   Outside a youth club

We see a sign 'Youth Club Dance Tonight – All Welcome' outside the entrance to the Youth Club. We hear **Mad Dog** *and* **Scully** *talking.*

Mad Dog: What're we gonna do now?

Scully: Hit anyone who says 'What are we gonna do now'?

[*We now see the boys outside the entrance, ready to go in. We see* **Joanna** *with three or four other girls sweep past them.* **Joanna** *walks towards where the Vicar is standing* *collecting the tickets and money. She turns and smiles at* **Scully** *briefly*]

Scully: All right, come 'head. An' try an' look holy . . .

[*We see* **Scully** *standing facing the Vicar in the club hallway. The others stand behind, portraying various shades of innocence*]

Scully: [*To the Vicar, humbly*] Yeah, I know it was a bit silly playin' table tennis with a billiard ball, Vicar, I can understand why we were banned, but to be honest now, Vicar, y' tables couldn't have been that strong.

Mooey: Er, I didn't play table tennis with the billiard balls, Victor.

Scully: No, you played head tennis an' spent the night in Casualty! [*He looks at the tight-lipped Vicar*] Come on boys, we know where we're not wanted. [*At the door*] It'll be a lousy dance anyway – who wants to hear a reggae version of the 23rd Psalm . . .

5 A road

We see the lads walking aimlessly along a road.

Mad Dog: What are we gonna do now?

Scully: We could go home.

Mad Dog: Wha'? Wha'? Go home, of a Friday night? *A Friday night!*

Scully: At least it doesn't rain in the house.

Mooey: It does in ours . . .

[*We see, approaching them,* **Mrs Scully** *and* **Gran***, linked onto each other, mainly to support* **Gran***. Hovering a distance behind are* **Gran's two elderly gents**]

Scully: All right Mam. What're y' doin'?

Mrs Scully: I'm tryin' to sober y' gran up before the pensioner's outin' an' then I'm goin' to the Parish Club.

Scully: On y' own?

Mrs Scully: No, Robert Redford's meetin' me outside at quarter to nine.

Scully: What about Mrs Barrett?

Mrs Scully: She's sick again.

Gran: I was sick again, but I'm better now. It's Blackpool tonight. I can't miss that.

Mad Dog: Blackpool. *Blackpool?*

Scully: Is there anyone in our house?

Mrs Scully: The usual – Arthur in mascara an' tights. Henry makin' train noises, an' Tony hopin' the others'll disappear so he can bring Rita back. [*She glances at* **Mooey;** **Mooey** *looks shifty*] And to think I always wanted sons . . . [*She starts to move off, but turns back to* **Scully**] An' you keep out of trouble, be home handy an' have a bath, d'y' hear?

[**Scully** *nods and turns away. We hear* **Mad Dog** *and the* **two elderly gents** *as the boys drift off*]

Mad Dog: Blackpool . . . Bloody Blackpool . . .

First elderly gent: Look Frank, she's sittin' with me on the coach comin' back, it's my turn anyway, you spent the afternoon with her in the Safari Park last week . . .

6   Mooey's house

We see **Mooey's** *house. It is surrounded by motorbikes.* **Mooey's** *door opens. We see* **Marie** *draped around the* **tattooed giant** *out of episode two. We hear rock music* *blasting, and we see Hell's Angels on the stairs.* **Marie** *winks and blows a kiss at* **Scully**. **Mooey** *winks and blows the kiss back.*

Mooey: Er hallo, Marie, er I'm home early, can I come in? Yis . . .

Tattooed giant: No.

[*The door slams in* **Mooey's** *face. He turns to the others*]

Mooey: Oh. Er, I can't come in, boys.

Scully: Tell them you're a poor orphan, Moo.

Mooey: Er, all right. [*He turns back, but gets dragged away before he goes to knock*]

7   Outside Scully's house

Scully *is hammering on the door. Lights come on in the hallway, and a dishevelled* **Tony** *arrives.*

Scully: What kept y'?

Tony: It's an excitin' part.

Scully: Where though? On the telly or with Rita, the Human Tractor?

Tony: You're lookin' for a good hidin'.

Scully: That'll be the day, Tony. The last time you give me one of them I was five an' you were thirteen.

Tony: What d' you want anyway?

Scully: We want to come in, we're short of a laugh.

Tony: Y' can't. [*He looks behind himself, and becomes more and more harassed*] Ah, come on, our kid, give us a break. I had to give Henry the train fare to Crewe Junction an' back to get rid of him and I've locked Arthur in me mam's wardrobe, mainly because he wanted me to, but go on, get lost will y'?

Scully: Say please.

Tony: Please. Please go.

Scully: [*Leaning on the doorframe*] No.

Tony: Here, here, I'll give y' a pound.

Scully: Each?

Tony: Between y', f'God's sake. Look here it is, now go on, push off.

Scully: [*Taking the pound*] Fair enough. I only came to get me ball anyway. [*He reaches around the door to get in*] Give Giant Haystacks my regards.

[**Tony** *goes to say something, then stops.* **Mooey** *has approached.* **Tony** *slams the door*]

8   Scully's road

We see **Scully**, **Mad Dog** *and* **Mooey** *running down* **Scully's** *road towards a corner house, kicking the ball and shouting.* **Snotty Dog** *is some way behind, kicking the pram and shouting. As they reach the corner house,* **Mooey** *approaches the bouncing ball.* **Scully** *shouts to him.*

Scully: No Mooey, *no!* [*Too late. The ball is hooked high into the sky.* **Mooey** *starts running after it*] 'Crackers'!

Mooey: [*In passing*] I'm not . . .

[*The ball lands in the path of the corner house. Before it can bounce a second time, we see* **Mrs 'Crackers' Leigh** *open her front door, catch the ball, turn happily and go inside, closing her door.* **Mooey** *stands in her path, not quite able to understand. He goes to the front door, bends down, lifts up the letterbox and peers inside. Two fingers come through the letterbox and jab him in the eyes. He howls and turns around*]

Mooey: Er, who was that?

Scully: Mrs Crackers ...

9   Outside a block of flats

We see the lads sitting on some bins at the back of a block of flats, eating a packet of chips each, but looking totally wet and dejected. Every so often **Snotty Dog** *slips the baby a chip.*

Mad Dog: Friday night ... I mean, *Friday night.*

Scully: It's like this every night, Mad Dog, never mind Fridays.

Mad Dog: I know. That's why I'm fed up.

Snotty Dog: [*Hopefully*] So am I.

Mooey: [*Happily*] So am I.

Mad Dog: I mean ... I mean ... I really feel like ... killin' someone. [**Snotty Dog** *edges away slightly*] It'll probably be meself. [**Snotty Dog** *edges back*] Look at us, no money, no place to go, no one to go there with. If I had money an' a job to go to when I left school, I'd have a girlfriend, and I'd be someone an' I'd be happy an' that. I might even have a car. One day when I get money.

[*As they sit there silently,* **Scully** *looks up and we see the* **caretaker** *of the flats approach.* **Scully** *scowls*]

Scully: Look out, Dunkirk. [*He look at us knowingly*]

[*We see a quick insert of a soldier in Second World War battle dress, armed to the teeth and approaching them in the zig-zag fashion, hiding behind whatever protection is available.*

We come back to reality and the lads as the **caretaker** *screams at them*]

Flat caretaker: You four, you four again, I'm fed up with you four comin' around here all the time, the four of you, causin' trouble, go on, gerrout of it, crawl back down the sewer y' came out of . . .

[*The lads look at each other, sitting peacefully on the bins. The* **caretaker** *hits* **Snotty Dog** *over the head as he arrives*]

Mad Dog: Ah sod off, Dunkirk, and leave our kid alone.

Flat caretaker: Don't you talk to me like that.

Scully: Yeah, I know you fought for the likes of us. An' y' haven't stopped regrettin' it since. Well, get lost, 'cos we weren't doin' nothin'. Not till you came.

[**Scully** *turns and kicks a bin over, scattering the contents.* **Mad Dog** *and* **Snotty Dog** *do the same.* **Mooey** *kicks at a bin and nearly breaks his foot. The* **caretaker** *starts chasing them away from the flats. Soon he stops, exhausted, and retreats to the flats muttering about the Welfare State. The lads start to follow him as he goes.*

We see them on their hands and knees as they sneak past the window and the door of the **caretaker's** *flat on the ground floor of the flats. They head towards the lifts in the 'foyer', crawling*]

Scully: Just one person to watch out for in here – the Mad Widow Mary . . .

Mooey: Who?

Scully: You'll see . . .

[*They get to the lifts.* **Snotty Dog** *struggles in with them despite* **Mad Dog's** *complaints. As the lift goes up, we see the* **caretaker's** *front door open very slightly*]

10   Inside the flats

We see the boys on the landing of the top floor of the flats, looking out over the estate and Liverpool.

Snotty Dog: All those lights.

Mooey: [*Sagely*] That's because it's night time. [*They all look at him and he nods at them*] Otherwise y' wouldn't be able to see them.

Mad Dog: So all right, we're here, this is obviously goin' to be the highlight of the night. So what are we gonna do now?

[**Scully** *turns towards* **Mad Dog,** *grins and knocks heavily on a front door*]

Scully: Give Mooey a treat . . .

Mooey: Yis . . .

[**Scully, Mad Dog** *and* **Snotty Dog** *move sideways away from the door to some sort of safety, as* **Mooey** *waits expectantly. The door opens. We cannot see the owner/ occupier*]

Mooey: Er, hallo . . . [*Looking down at waist level*] Er . . . I never knocked on your door, I'm only here for a treat an' er . . . [*He turns and points*] 'n' to look at the lights. [*Turning back*] Er, I'm a poor orphan but, er, I haven't got any trees at the moment.

[*We see* **Mooey** *getting hit over the head with a baseball bat. He sinks to the floor and looks up. We see a very old lady as she stands over him with a baseball bat in her hands and a very determined expression on her face. She closes the door without a word.* **Mooey** *looks up at* **Scully** *and the others*]

Scully: That was er, Mad Widow Mary, Moo.

Mooey: Er yeah, er she doesn't like orphans much, does she ... either that, or she hates trees ...

Scully: Well, here, Moo, see what this one thinks.

[*He bangs on another door, and runs.* **Mad Dog** *gallops, and* **Snotty Dog** *and pram charge off.* **Mooey** *stays and waits, practising*]

Mooey: Er hallo, er I'm *not* a poor orphan, and I can't stand trees ... er hallo, er ...

[*He gets bored waiting and knocks on the door himself. As he does so,* **Scully** *comes back, laughing, and hauls him away. We see them running along the landing, knocking on all the doors as they go. They reach the lifts.* **Mad Dog**, **Scully** *and* **Mooey** *pile in.* **Mad Dog** *presses the button and closes the door as* **Snotty Dog** *gets there.* **Snotty Dog** *bangs on the lift door, turns and sees some angry tenants approaching on the landing. He bangs again, and looks back. Meanwhile the lift opens.* **Snotty Dog** *keeps on banging, and hits* **Mooey** *right in the face.* **Mad Dog** *pulls* **Snotty Dog** *and* **Snotty Dog** *pulls the pram. The lift door closes as we fade on* **Mooey** *holding his head.*]

11   Inside the lift

We see the boys in the lift. For the first time they are full of life and laughing. Even the baby may be laughing. They reach the ground floor. The lift doesn't immediately open. **Scully** *hits the 'open' button and pushes at the door. They glance at each other, and the door opens as we hear the* **caretaker's** *cackling laugh.* **Isaiah** *and another policeman stand framed in the doorway.*

Mooey: Er, good evening, Isaiah, I've never been a poor orphan ...

[*The scene fades*]

12   A police interview room

We see **Isaiah** *and the boys, and a* **policewoman** *walking a pram up and down the corridor.* **Isaiah** *closes the door and approaches* **Mooey.**

Isaiah: An' what were *you* doin'?

Mooey: I was with them. I think. [*Looking out of the corner of his eye*] That's right, I recognize them.

Isaiah: I could throw the book at you for this y' know.

Mooey: [*Quietly*] I can't read.

Isaiah: You were in there with intent to steal. A serious offence. A puttin' away offence for one or two of you. Those of you with records. [*He looks at* **Scully**]

Mooey: I've got a cassette player.

[**Isaiah** *prods* **Mooey,** *almost without looking, and pushes him so that his chair falls back.* **Mooey** *keeps talking as he gets up*]

Mooey: But I have. It needs batteries, an' er, I haven't actually got any cassettes, but –

[**Isaiah** *raises his hand, and* **Mooey** *huddles away from him.* **Isaiah** *focuses on* **Scully** *mainly. He means every word.* **Mooey** *moves forward enthusiastically as* **Isaiah** *talks*]

Isaiah: I'll have you. Good an' proper. Make no mistake. Your kind, you're all the same, seen one, you've seen them all. An' I have seen them all on this estate, whole families of them. I just have to look into your eyes, it's all there, that's where it is – y' eyes – trickery, lyin', deceit, plain thuggery an' violence. Y' eyes tell me all that an' more. I can see y' future planned out right there. And –

Mooey: Er, can y' read palms as well?

[**Mooey** *gets knocked off his chair again.* **Scully** *looks at* **Isaiah** *with hatred. He looks at us. He half smiles finally, and nods towards* **Isaiah**. *We see* **Isaiah** *dressed as a female fortune teller with a crystal ball, for the next speech only*]

Isaiah: An' I know as sure as night follows day what lies ahead of you lot – even that bloody baby outside – petty crimes, a little muggin', a few burglaries, Borstal, gaol, in an' out of courtrooms an' prison yards all y' empty slimy little lives –

Mooey: He's good, isn't he? [*The others cannot look at* **Mooey**] Just by lookin' in our eyes – flippin' heck! [*He gets closer to* **Isaiah** *and opens his eyes wide*] Can y' see anythin' else? A gypsy once told me mam that I was going to be the next prime min–

Isaiah: [*Back in uniform now, still prodding* **Mooey** *as he talks*] Shut it, you, I'm not interested in you. The likes of you should have been put down at birth. Either that, or your father shouldn't have bothered.

Mooey: [*With considerable genuine dignity*] That's not a very nice thing to say. My dad's got nothin' to do with me.

Isaiah: An' I'll tell you all somethin' else for free – if I ever so much as see you doin' anythin' suspicious again, I don't care what I have to do, I don't care if I have to make the evidence fit the crime, I'll get you put away. Understand?

Mad Dog: But y' can't do that! [**Isaiah** *stands heavily on* **Mad Dog**'s *feet*] Yes y' can, y' can do anythin' y' want, I just forgot f' a minute.

Scully: [*Really fed-up*] I've had enough of this.

Isaiah: Oh really?

Scully: Yeah, I have. If y' goin' to do somethin', do it. Y' know what I mean. 'Cos I tell y', y' can't really hurt us – y' won't even beat us up – we weren't doin' nothin' in those flats, nothin' that was worth doin', an' you know it. So listen, either book us, batter us or let us go back to doin' what we were doin'. Which was nothin' much. [**Scully** *stands up*] All right?

[*Pause*]

Isaiah: Get out, go on. But just let me catch you, that's all.

[**Scully** *smirks at him. They all leave, and go into the corridor. The policewoman gives the pram to* **Mad Dog**, *who refuses to accept it.* **Snotty Dog** *takes it. They walk on*]

13   Outside the police station

Mad Dog: You were brave in there, weren't you?

Scully: I know, but he can't touch me, an' all that he said isn't goin' to happen to me. [**Mad Dog** *looks at him*] I'm goin' to be a footballer, aren't I?

[*He walks on. We just catch* **Mad Dog's** *cynicism*]

14   The local streets

We see the boys once more on a walkabout – it is late, late evening.

Scully: Well, all it leaves is your house, Mad Dog.

Mad Dog: There's no room.

Scully: We don't want bed an' breakfast. We just want somewhere to go out of the rain.

Snotty Dog: We can't go back home yet, me mam's got all her friends round.

Scully: Well that room won't be crowded.[*The* **Dogs** *look puzzled but let it go*] Where's your dad then?

Mad Dog: [*Looking away*] I was hopin' you wouldn't ask that.

Scully: Why?

Mad Dog: 'Cos that's him over there in those privets ... [*The boys look across the road towards the privets surrounding a garden. A man is half into them trying to pull out another man, who has gone right through them. As he does so, we see both men*] ... with your dad.

Mr O'Gorman: Come on Alfie ... y' won't like it down there ... let's start again hey? [*He sings*] 'The Green Green Grass of Home ...'

Mr Scully: Don't sing that song George, it ... it makes me cry ...

[**Scully** *helps his father up as both men fall down again. The* **Dogs** *struggle with their father.* **Mr Scully** *throws his arms at* **Scully**]

Mr Scully: Fra ... Francis, oh Francis, tell me ... tell me y've come to take me home, Francis. [*Nearly pulling* **Scully** *down*]

Scully: Yeah, I'll take y' home dad, but not to our house. I'm in enough trouble already with me mam.

Mr Scully: [*As they limp along towards the house that* **Mr Scully** *now lives in*] She won't wash for me, this one, y' know, nothin' ... she burns everythin' she touches an' the house is dirty, Francis ... she ... she just uses me body, that's all, just uses me –

Scully: All right Dad, flippin' hell ...

Mr Scully: Tell y' mam ... y' know tell her I still love her, Francis, still.

Scully: Here y' are dad. [*He leans him against the front gate. The others carry on towards the* **Dogs'** *house*]

Mr Scully: An' . . . she said she'd wash for me, she said . . . an' she's ugly, Francis . . . ugly . . .

Scully: See y', dad. [*Goes off towards the others*]

Mr Scully: [*Calling after* **Scully** *as he goes*] You don't know how ugly she is . . . she's so ugly! She – [*We hear him faintly but clearly*] Oh hallo, love, I was . . . was just talkin' about you . . .

15   The Dogs' House

We see a key trying to go into a keyhole. Eventually, the door opens. **Mr O'Gorman** *staggers into the house.* **Mad Dog, Scully** *and* **Mooey** *follow him in.*

16   Inside the Dogs' House

Mad Dog *indicates to them to be quiet as they stand in the hallway.* **Mr O'Gorman** *takes out a large, almost full bottle of red wine, and gives it to* **Mad Dog.**

Mr O'Gorman: Here, son, hide that for me. I told your mother I had no money before.

[*He staggers up the stairs, and hiccups as he goes.* **Mad Dog** *gives the bottle to* **Scully,** *who gives it to* **Mooey**]

Mooey: Yis! Red lemonade, my favourite!

[*There is a knock on the front door.* **Scully** *opens it, and we see* **Snotty Dog** *looking pathetically in, still with the pram. They let him in. He takes the baby and goes upstairs with it, as* **Mad Dog, Mooey** *and* **Scully** *tiptoe towards the living room*]

17   The Dogs' living room

We see a darkened living room. Five middle-aged women are huddled around the table with their fingers ready and a glass in the middle. Another is kneeling in the light from the imitation log fire. We see **Mad Dog** *peep in, and motion with his lips.* **Scully** *and* **Mooey** *sneak in and sit on the floor in the furthest corner.* **Mrs O'Gorman,** *her back turned to the door, speaks in a piercing 'Seance' voice, with an attempt to be posh as well.*

Mrs O'Gorman: Right ladies, I'd like to start with the board now, do' you mind not smokin', Mrs McGuffin, they don't like it, y' know. Thank you, now you see before you this Zodiac Glass that was bequeened to me by mother's Aunty Florrie who had gypsy blood an' she was the seventh daughter of the seventh mother an' she left it to me when she passed on, so we could keep in touch, like. Just rest y' finger on it now, girls, so y' can get familiar with it . . .

Scully: [*Whispers*] She takes it all a bit serious, doesn't she?

Mad Dog: So would you, Scull, if you'd seen her in action. She's been talkin' to a cabin boy off the *Titanic* for years, little Billy McGinty.

Scully: Does y' dad know she's got another feller?

Mrs O'Gorman: [*To the woman at the fire*] Got enough light there for the messages Freda? Right. Now any questions before we start?

Scully: [*As someone asks a question in the background*] This is daft. I think I'd rather be out in the rain.

Mad Dog: It's not, you know Scull. What about this – the last time Billy McGinty came over from the other side, he spelt out the words – 'Alice Jones dead'!

Mooey: But, er hey, Mad Dog, er like Alice Jones, er she isn't dead. She's just gone to the Parish Club with our Valerie.

Mad Dog: Yeah, I know but the day after me mam got that message, her twin brother got his head trapped in a spin dryer at Long Bow Launderette an' had one of his ears torn off!

Mooey: [*Getting hold of* **Scully's** *arm*] Oooooh!

Mrs O'Gorman: Of course you can ask about y' own folk up there, Joan, Billy'll be only too happy to find out for you. Right now, here we go, I want you to concentrate on someone who's passed away, someone what's gone, departed to the other world . . . y' know kicked the bucket – just try and picture them in y'mind, think back to the happy times y' used to have. [*There is a long pause, and a couple of bronchial coughs*] Is anyone there? Is . . . anyone . . . there?

Mooey: [*As if to the deaf*] Er, yes missus – I'm here!

[*There are a couple of screams and giggles to release the tension, but not from* **Mrs O'Gorman**]

Mrs O'Gorman: [*Coming over*] Did you let them in, Graham, did you? Go on, go up to your room an' get rid of the others, you know no spirits'll come if there's unbelievers in the room, they know y' only there for a laugh an' they don't come, they go elsewhere.

Mad Dog: [*Going out*] But we won't mess, Mam, honest . . .

Mrs O'Gorman: It doesn't matter, Billy's very fussy about who he talks to, an' you know what happened last year when Marie Lloyd was just about to give us a song an' y' father was sick all over the alphabet, never saw hide nor hair of her again . . .

[*She slams the door, and we see the lads in the doorway, going towards the front door*]

18 The O'Gorman's hall

Mad Dog: What are we gonna do now?

[**Snotty Dog** *comes down the stairs*]

Snotty Dog: I've er, got –

Scully: Home James, that's what we do –

Snotty Dog: No y' see, I've got an idea.

Mad Dog: Shut it, you, Snotty, it's all your fault. [*He hits him*]

Scully: [*Opening the front door*] See y'.

Snotty Dog: Why don't we go up to our loft like we do when we're waggin' school?

[*They are about to ignore him when they realize it's the best idea of the night*]

Scully: Have you had a brain transplant? That's a crackin' idea.

Snotty Dog: I know.

Mad Dog: I was just going to suggest it, as a matter of fact.

Scully: Lead the way, squire . . .

19 The loft

We see the loft. There is a mattress across the beams, a gas lantern, some cups, plates, etc., and a big picture of Kenny Dalglish across the beams. **Scully** *glances at it, glances at us, and then whispers to Dalglish.*

Scully: An' don't you say a word . . . [*We hear snoring from below – heavy snoring*] Who's that snoring?

Snotty Dog: It's me dad.

[*We see* **Mooey** *drinking hugely from the wine bottle*]

Scully: Sounds like a foggy night on the Mersey . . .

Mooey: [*Offering the bottle of wine with a hiccup*] Er anyone want any of this red lemonade? [*He takes another swig. The others grin knowingly*] It er, doesn't taste much like Tizer to me though . . .

Mad Dog: Do you think he knows what he's drinking?

Scully: [*As* **Mooey** *starts humming and then singing 'Liverpool'*] Nah, no chance. An' y' know what he's like – eats two ounces of wine gums an' he goes all dizzy an' has to sit down.

Mooey: [*Spaced out*] Ooooooh, I don't half feel smart . . . [*He starts to stand up, reaches up, takes a Liverpool scarf off the beams, and starts singing, painfully*] 'We hate Nottingham Forest, we hate Everton too . . .' [*He goes through the song, waving about but staying well on the mattress. He finishes the song, and drinks again, the scarf draped around his hands. He offers the others a drink*] Er, when's the kick-off, Scull?

Scully: The wha'?

Mooey: The . . . the er . . . kick-off. Er when're the teams comin' out? I've been standin' here ages . . . it must be er . . . three o'clock now.

Scully: Evenin' kick-off, Moo.

Mooey: Oh aye yeah. [*He gets the bottle back, and has another swig and takes his first big stagger. He burps, and starts to sing at the top of his voice*] 'We hate Nottingham Forest . . .'

Scully: Take it easy, Moo.

Mad Dog: Yeah, stay still will y'?

Mooey: '. . . We hate Everton too . . .' [*He spins for the first time*]

[*The others get on their knees around him, trying to stop him going off the mattress, and he starts jumping up and down. He falls down towards the mattress, does a complete forward roll and finds himself on the beams, just as he reaches the final words of the song*]

Mooey: '. . . But Liverpool we love you . . .'[*He is soaked in wine*]

Scully: Look out, you're going to –

[**Mooey** *topples, a dead weight again, perhaps in the hope of another forward roll. The others lean forward, with their hands out.* **Mooey** *crashes through the beams onto the bed. The bedroom floor collapses, the end of the bed tips down and* **Mooey** *slides off through the floor on to the seance table below.* **Mr O'Gorman** *clings to the bed*]

Scully: – fall through the ceiling.

[*We see the terrifying hole, and* **Snotty Dog** *already trying to climb out of the loft window*]

Snotty Dog: Me dad'll kill me.

Mad Dog: What are we going to do now?

[**Scully** *edges towards the hole and looks down. We see the plaster and the dust settling into a haze below them.* **Mr O'Gorman** *is in his beer-gut vest and undies, still far from sober or awake. He can't work out what has happened*]

20   The living room

The women see **Mooey** *spread-eagled on the table, white-faced and big-eyed. They too just stare at* **Mooey** *for a second.*

Mrs O'Gorman: It's him! It's him! It's Billy McGinty of the *Titanic*, Glory be to God, I've brought him down.

Mooey: [*Climbing off the table*] No, it's er . . . simple, look . . . [*The women about-turn and run off screaming,* **Mooey** *following them out*] Er no, hang on, ere I'm a bit scared meself, er don't go without me . . .

[*He follows them – we see* **Scully** *on the stairs tip-toeing towards the front door*]

21 The hall

Mooey *is in the hall, outside the door leading to the kitchen.*

Mooey: Er, wha're y'all doin' in the toilet, girls . . . [*A few whimpers*] Arra, go on, tell me . . .]Someone starts sobbing]

Mrs O'Gorman: [*From inside the crowded toilet*] Where's Freda? Is Freda here?

A Woman: [*From inside*] I think she dived under the stairs.

22 The cupboard under stairs

It opens from the outside. We see a distraught **Freda** *huddled in there.*

Mooey: [*Ever helpful*] Er, is your name Freda?

Freda: Oh God, don't touch me.

Mooey: Er no, er them women, er, they want y' to go in the toilet. [*He goes to let her out*] Er go an' ask them if I can come with y', hey, go on.

Freda: Aagghh! He touched me, he touched me!

23   Outside the house

Outside the house, **Scully**, **Mad Dog** *and* **Snotty Dog** *are by the gate.*

Mr O'Gorman: [*To* **Mad Dog** *and* **Snotty Dog**] Were you two part of this? *Were you?* [*He lifts up both of them by the scruff of their jackets*]

Scully: Well, Mad Dog, what I want to know is – what are you going to do now? [*He grins at the lads, then at us, and walks away. We see him walking away as* **Mooey** *arrives beside him, puffed out.* **Scully** *looks at us as he walks, and* **Mooey** *turns and walks along with him*] Just a normal kind of night ... Still, there's one good thing about tonight, I haven't had any time to think, and I haven't once seen things that aren't there – like Kenny Dalglish.

[*We move back from him as he finishes talking. We see that indeed he is walking along not with* **Mooey** *but with* **Kenny Dalglish.** **Scully** *walks for some time without noticing, then turns casually towards* **Mooey.** *He sees* **Dalglish,** *and stops dead in his tracks. We freeze on* **Scully's** *bewildered look*]

Episode 5

Scully, Mooey and Mad Dog discover a lot of balls in Mrs 'Crackers' Leigh's bathroom

Episode 5

---

1 Steve's classroom

*It is twelve o'clock, and we see remnants of classes running down the corridor. There is silence. **Steve** is putting his science apparatus away. He lights his pipe. There is a human skeleton on the wall between the door and **Steve's** preparation desk at the front of the classroom. There is a knock on the half-open door. We see **Scully** in the doorway, standing diffidently. He glances around the room, as if looking for someone. He moves towards a stool at the side of **Steve's** desk, and sits down.*

Steve: Look, I'll do a deal with you.

Scully: [*Puzzled*] What?

Steve: It's simple. All I want is –

[**Steve** *glances towards the doorway. We see **Dracula** and **Castanets** at the doorway, smiling sweetly. **Dracula** has a large brush and **Castanets** has a dust-pan*]

Steve: Yes?

Dracula: [*Edging into the room as he talks*] Anything need brushing up, Mr Stevens?

Castanets: Mr Stevens.

Dracula: The remnants of any experiments that I can dispense with? The odd bull's eye or rat's stomach? [*He laughs warmly and practises his sweeping*]

Castanets: Rat's stomach.

Steve: Not today.

Dracula: [*Motioning*] A little sweep here and there?

Castanets: There.

Steve: Not now. [*Firmly*] Thank you.

Castanets: Thank you.

[**Dracula** *sulks for a split second, then smiles at* **Scully**. *He moves towards the door, followed by* **Castanets**. *He is near to the skeleton.*

We see **Scully** *look at him sourly, and then glance at us. We see* **Dracula** *from* **Scully's** *point of view, dressed as 'Dracula', his cape swirling as he savages the skeleton's neck for a second. He moves away from the skeleton and spits out a bit of neck bone.*

We come back to reality and to **Steve** *and* **Scully** *as we hear the door closing behind* **Castanets** *and* **Dracula**]

Steve: As I was saying, I want to do a deal with you.

[**Scully** *puts his head on his folded arms and speaks through them*]

Scully: Big deal!

Steve: You don't know the deal.

Scully: [*Sitting up*] Oh aye? Really? Whatever the deal is, it has to involve actin'. An' that's no deal at all. I don't want to wear make-up an' lipstick an' learn lines, I can't do falsetto, an' I don't want to knock around with Handbags Anonymous. All right?

[**Scully** *stands and turns away. He sees* **Mrs Heath** *coming out of the stock room, smoking the inevitable cigarette.* **Scully** *sighs*]

Scully: Ah well, it wouldn't be a show without Punch.

Mrs Heath: We won't ask you again.

Scully: Promise?

Steve: Yes.

Scully: Great. The answer's no. [*He turns again towards the door. He is near the skeleton. He notices a piece of neck bone on the desk by the skeleton. He looks momentarily puzzled as he picks it up*]

Steve: Pity. Part of the deal was a trial with Liverpool.

[**Scully** *stops at the door, his back turned to* **Steve** *and* **Mrs Heath**]

Scully: Liverpool what?

Steve: What else? Liverpool Football Club.

Scully: [*Turning around*] We've gone up in the world, haven't we? You only used to promise me a trial with Blackburn Rovers.

Steve: I never *promised* you anything.

Scully: You are now though. Aren't you?

Steve: [*Shrugs*] It'll sort out how good you really are. Then we'll know.

Scully: And then I'll go in the pantomime?

Steve: Yes.

Scully: No.

Mrs Heath: Oh come on.

Scully: [*Firmly*] *No*. If I'm good enough, you'll take me for a trial anyway, or I'll get one meself – Liverpool or Blackburn Rovers or whoever – an' so actin' an' pantomimes don't come into it, do they?

Mrs Heath: [*Lightly*] Well, once again, you know all the answers, Scully . . . even if they are the wrong ones.

[**Scully** *looks at her, grins and turns away. As he gets to the* *door, we hear* **Dalglish's** *voice*]

Dalglish: But the question is, are you good enough?

[**Scully** *turns – we see* **Dalglish** *where* **Mrs Heath** *was, staring with absolute disgust at the cigarette in his hand. He throws it away, and looks at* **Scully**]

Scully: Oh this is gettin' out of hand!

[*He shakes his head, opens the door and marches away. We see* **Steve** *limping after him*]

2   The school corridor

Finally **Steve** *stops* **Scully** *as* **Scully** *approaches a corner where* **Dracula** *is brushing a litter-free floor, while* **Castanets** *stoops with his dust-pan.*

Steve: Scully . . . Scully!

Scully: Array, Steve. Come on – [*Pointing at his own head*] It's doin' me head in, this. Do me a favour. You know I don't want to do it.

Steve: Four o'clock. Think about it this afternoon, and tell me at four o'clock. I'll be in my room.

[**Steve** *turns away, and limps back towards his room.* **Scully** *leans against a window frame, watching him go. He glances the other way down the corridor, and sees* **Dracula** *and* **Castanets** *edging very near.* **Scully** *turns and looks out of the window*]

Dracula: Hallo Francis.

Castanets: Francis.

Dracula: Nice day for it, hey?

Castanets: Hey. Hey? [*He looks out of the window*] But it's raining, Wally.

[**Dracula** *hits him quietly and savagely with his broom handle in the stomach, just before* **Scully** *turns around and faces them*]

Scully: Look, what do you want?

Dracula: Me? 'What do I want?' I want nothing, nothing at all.

Castanets: All.

Scully: [*Swinging off the window-sill*] And that's what you're going to get. [*Walking past them*] I don't know what's goin' on, Dracula, but stay away.

[*We watch* **Scully** *walk around a corner, and hear* **Castanets** *talking to* **Dracula** . . .]

Castanets: Er, why do they call you Dracula, Wally? [*A vicious sound of blood being sucked*] Oooow!

3 The school canteen

Scully *turns to his school dinner and contemplates a pilchard. He sees Joanna's friends leaving the table. Both* **Scully** *and* **Joanna** *are now on their own. We watch him for a bit as he quietly fidgets and looks sly-eyed, till they look at each other, across two empty dinner tables.* **Scully** *finally takes his almost finished dinner and his semolina across to her. He sits down, stilted and nervous.*

Scully: Hiya! Joanna. [*He pretends to look all around and under the table. She looks at him*] Just lookin' for Mooey. [*She laughs. They carry on eating for a while*] . . . Er, how's it goin'?

Joanna: The pantomime?

Scully: No! Just . . . everything, you know . . . how's it goin'?

Joanna: All right. The pantomime's great though. I'm in the running for –

Scully: Oh hey! [*Pushing his pilchards away*]

Joanna: What's the matter?

Scully: Oh nothin' – just the brainwashin' – you know – I was in Woolies yesterday an' three girls behind the counter told me how good the pantomime was. [*He reaches for his semolina*] Two of them asked me why I wasn't doin' it, an' the other one pulled out a script. [*Silence*] . . . I er, didn't come over here to talk about that anyway . . . I er . . . [*He looks away, and reaches towards where the sugar, salt and pepper cellars are. He takes hold of the salt cellar, and begins to pour salt on his semolina.* **Joanna** *notices. He doesn't*] . . . like you know . . . I was just wonderin' . . .

Joanna: [*Finally*] Do you know you're pouring salt on your semolina?

Scully: Er . . . yeah, oh aye, yeah. [*Adds some more*] I er, like it like that. [*He takes a mouthful and quietly chokes on it; then looks up and smiles*] I was, er . . . just wonderin', Joanna, if there was any date of a chance. [*He closes his eyes*] . . . Chance of a date? [*He takes a mouthful of semolina, and then another. Both look away*]

Joanna: I'd like to Franny, but I won't have much time for the next few weeks. With the pantomime you know.

Scully: The bloody pantomime! [*Long pause*] So y' saying no.

Joanna: No. I'm not sayin' no.

Scully: It doesn't sound like 'Yes' to me. And it definitely isn't remotely like 'How about tonight!'

Joanna: But it still isn't 'No'. It's . . . 'Not yet, but maybe later.'

Scully: [*Standing*] It'll be too late then, girl. Y' only get one chance with me. And you've just missed it. There's plenty more fish in the sea. [*He walks away with his semolina*]

Joanna: [*Quietly*] But who wants to kiss a fish?

4   Steve's classroom

We hear a bell going for the end of afternoon school. We see **Steve**'s *room.* **Steve** *is at the window, his back turned. He lights his pipe and glances at his watch.*

*   **Steve** *gets closer to the window and stares down intently. Then he glances around as* **Mrs Heath** *enters the room.* **Steve** *indicates quietly out of the window. They both look down. From their point of view, we see* **Scully**, *with* **Mad Dog** *and* **Brian Bignall** *and a few others sauntering away from school.* **Scully** *never looks back.*

5   Outside a public house

We see **Scully** *leaving the others and crossing a road, approaching a public house. There is a figure of a man on the steps, sitting slumped, head between hands.* **Scully** *gets closer to him: it is* **Mr Scully.**

Scully: Array Dad, it's only ten past four.

Mr Scully: There's nowhere to go, son. Nowhere worth going. There's only two places I want to go anymore . . . and I only go in one 'cos I'm not allowed in the other . . . tell y' mam, Francis, tell her I'd give anything to go back . . . Let me come back.

Scully: Dad! You know . . . it's not up to me, it's up to me mam, and the last time I mentioned it, I nearly didn't live there neither.

Mr Scully: [*Not listening*] Y' know what they call her in there, the one I'm with now – they call her 'Buried Treasure'...'cos everytime they see me with her, they say 'Where did y' dig her up'...I'm not kiddin', son...I'm... [*Putting his head down*] ... not.

Scully: [*To himself*] Jeez! [*He walks away*]

6 Scully's kitchen

We see **Scully** *in the back kitchen of his house, facing the window above the sink.* **Mrs Scully** *is there.*

Scully: I'm just tellin' y', Mam. That's all.

Mrs Scully: And I'm tellin' you as well.

Scully: But neither of us're listenin'.

Mrs Scully: What do you mean by that?

Scully: [*Shaking his head*] He's killin' himself. Nothin' more, nothin' less.

Mrs Scully: He's been doin' it for twenty-five years an' he's not dead yet.

Scully: But he's me dad.

Mrs Scully: He was.

Scully: [*Suddenly roused*] He still is!

[*Long pause*]

Mrs Scully: Yes. He is. I'm sorry. But that's *all* I am.

[**Mrs Scully** *goes to the chip pan and turns the gas on.* **Scully** *slowly goes out*]

7 The living room

Scully *enters the living room. He sees* **Henry** *reading a* *railway magazine,* **Arthur** *glued to a fashion parade on the television, and* **Gran** *sat on the couch with a wet flannel on her head. Sitting either side of her are* **Tony** *and* **Mrs Barrett**, *staring out in a state of quiet shock.* **Scully** *looks at them, and then looks at us. Flatly, he turns about and goes out of the door. He goes into the hallway and straight out of the front door.*

8 Mooey's road

We see **Scully** *as he walks down* **Mooey's** *road, towards* **Mooey's** *house.* **Joanna's** *house is a couple of houses further up.* **Marie** *is at the door of her house and a motorbike is roaring and screaming away from the pavement.* **Mooey** *is at the gate, holding his ears and shouting.*

Mooey: Can I come in now, Marie? [*He sees* **Scully**] Er, it's all right, I don't want to, the couch is ruined anyway. Where y' goin', Scully? Can I come? Only er, I don't want to go to Mad Dog's, they don't like me there anymore.

[**Marie** *is advancing towards the gate*]

Scully: I'm going to Mad Dog's.

Mooey: [*Promptly*] I'll take a chance.

Scully: Later Moo, I'm not in the mood.

Marie: Why don't you come in, Francis, seeing as he doesn't want to. [*She leans across the gate*] Maybe we could have a little 'mood' together.

Mooey: Er, I'm easy, I don't mind, the er, couch isn't that bad, apart from the engine oil.

Scully: Look, all I want to do is – [*He sees* **Joanna** *walking along the pavement towards them, still some distance away.* **Scully** *moves towards the gate and* **Marie**. *He bumps into* **Mooey** *as he tries to get there first. He moves him aside*] – inspect that couch of yours, Marie, and its contents.

Mooey: I found five pee down there once.

Scully: The contents of the couch when you're sitting there, Marie.

[**Joanna** *is about fifteen yards away.* **Scully** *is close to* **Marie**]

Marie: Oh the boy has such a way with words.

Mooey: Yeah, it's er, called sentences. We're doin' them in sch –

Marie: [*Viciously*] Shut it you!

Mooey: Sorry Marie. [*He stands there, and sees* **Joanna** *sweeping past*] Er, hallo girl. Er, I'm still captain, but I've packed up bein' an orphan. Er, d' you wanna see our couch, er . . . [*She walks past, and glances at* **Scully**. *She smiles over her shoulder in an amused fashion as* **Scully** *breathes all over* **Marie**]

Scully: Oh hiya, Joanna, didn't see you there . . . See you. Then.

[**Joanna** *keeps walking.* **Scully** *can't help watching her – until his head is jerked back by both* **Marie's** *hands to face her*]

Marie: Mmmmm, don't tell me I've got competition. [*She fondles his hair*] Ohhhh, if only there wasn't a gate between us.

[**Scully** *glances at* **Joanna's** *door, and sees her looking as she goes in – he is jerked back to look at* **Marie**]

Scully: I know, we'll have to do something about it – we can't keep meeting like this.

Mooey: I can get rid of the gate for y', if y' want.

Scully: Mooey, can I ask you a question? [**Mooey** *nods*] Would you like to go away?

[**Mooey** *considers the question carefully*]

Mooey: Er ... er ... no! [*He looks eagerly at* **Scully** *and* **Marie**] Did I get it right? [**Marie** *and* **Scully** *shake their heads gravely*] ... Oh. Er, OK. Er d' y' wanna ask me an easier one? [*They shake their heads again*] Y' can ask me another hard one if y' want. [*They look daggers at him. He flinches away*] All right then, I'll go. [*But he hovers at the door, listening if he can*]

Marie: Alone at last. Can it last?

Scully: [*Breaking away, laughing*] Oh-hey, Marie, you're all mouth.

Marie: [*Pouting*] Don't you like my mouth, Francis?

Scully: Yeah, it's fine, it's in the right place, underneath y' nose, on top of y' chin.

Marie: Wouldn't you like a closer inspection ...

Scully: All right, all right, look – put up or shut up – meet me tonight, half past seven outside the 'Bow an' Arrow'. An' then we'll know.

Marie: I can't.

Scully: See – there you are. Y' bluff's called. So –

Marie: I can't see you *tonight* but I can tomorrow. Same time, same place. Don't be late. [**Scully** *looks at her.* **Mooey** *has sneaked nearby*] Whose bluff's bein' called now, Francis? [*She pinches his cheek, and she turns away*] Take me somewhere ... exciting ... loverboy.

Mooey: Er, can y' take me as well, lov – er, Scully?

Scully: [*To* **Marie**] OK. You're on.

Mooey: Yis! Ta Scull. I haven't been anywhere excitin' f' yonks ...

Marie: [*As we fade, and* **Marie** *takes hold of* **Mooey** *by the neck*] Mooey, there's something you need to be told ... [*She moves him towards the house*]

9   The Leighs' house

We see **Scully** *and* **Mad Dog,** *standing underneath a lamp-post outside what we will later discover to be the Leighs' house.*

Mad Dog: There's nothing to do.

Scully: [*Angrily*] There's never nothing to do! We know that. It's an established fact.

Mad Dog: Yeah. I wanna do something big, Scull. Y' know ... big. Like ... In these days of unemployment and recession.

Scully: Wha'?

Mad Dog: In these days of unemployment and recession. It was on the news before I came out. That and a war somewhere. But if I did something big ... people would notice me.

Scully: I think I'll go home.

Mad Dog: No one notices me at home. Except when the ceilin' falls in.

Scully: I'll be able to leave home soon.

Mad Dog: They still wouldn't notice. I wanna be noticed wherever I go. Recognized. An' I don't wanna be called Mad Dog f' the rest of me life. I don't wanna be a pensioner called Mad Dog O'Gorman.

[*There is a silence, broken in the distance by* **Snotty Dog** *running happily towards them from one direction and* **Mooey** *running from another*]

Snotty Dog: [*As he advances*] I got rid of the pram, boys – I got rid of it [*He laughs and rubs his hands together.* **Scully** *casually feels in* **Snotty Dog**'*s jacket pocket.* **Snotty Dog** *pulls his jacket away. He speaks slightly too quickly*] I haven't got any money, honest.

Scully: I was just lookin' for the baby.

Snotty Dog: He's with the pram.

[**Mooey** *arrives on the scene, happy too*]

Mooey: All right boys, er, hey Scull, er y'know that somewhere-excitin' that y'takin' me an' Marie tomorrow?

Scully: If bread was brains, Moo, you'd starve to death.

Mooey: What do you mean?

Mad Dog: Somewhere special?

Snotty Dog: [*Laughing*] With Marie Morgan? Uurrgghh!

[*There is lots of laughter and taunts.* **Scully** *bounces* **Mad Dog** *through the Leighs' privets, and chases* **Snotty Dog**. *He bangs him against the gate, and out bounce* **Mrs 'Crackers' Leigh** *and* **Mr 'Crackers'**. *She thinks herself much superior to her neighbours*]

Mrs Crackers: [*All in one breath*] I've had enough of you lot what do you think you're doing standing there go and stand by your own lamp-post haven't you got better things to do where 're your parents that's what I want to know what are they doing how would they like it if you stood outside *their* house all night long. Hey? [*Deep intake of breath*] I've watched you lot day in and day out for nigh on twenty years –

Mooey: Er, I'm only sixteen.

Scully: Yeah, yeah, all right, and we've heard it all before, very good, without doubt a sanctimonious fit of the first order, Crackers –

Mrs Crackers: [*Shouting*] Don't call me Crackers!

Scully: Sorry, Fruitcake –

Mrs Crackers: [*To her husband*] Malcolm!

Scully: But listen, take me, I'd be very happy if I had somethin' to do and I wasn't standin' here listenin' to this –

but y' know why I have to stand here – because I've got
nothin' else to do – and you know why I haven't got anythin'
else to do?

Mooey: 'Cos our Marie isn't here.

Scully: [*To* **Mrs Crackers**] Because I like playin' football.
But I haven't got a ball to play with. An' you know
why?

Mooey: Er, I don't think our Marie's got anythin' t' do with
this.

Scully: [*Still to* **Mrs Crackers**] Because you've got the
only decent caseball I had – because you've got balls in
your house belongin' to blokes with beer bellies now.
Because standin' there behind y' net curtains waitin' for a
ball to come over or a crowd to form is y' only bit of fun in
life, isn't it? Y' wouldn't want to live anywhere else would
y'? 'Cos y' like it here – the King of the Castle, Lord an'
Lady Muck, lookin' down on the rest of us. D' y' know what
youse are, do y'? Y' worse than any of us, worse than
anyone around here. You're a pair of . . . [*He can't think of
the word*]

Mooey: Er, hypocrites.

Scully: Yeah, that's the wor – hypo – [*Double take at*
Mooey] – crites. An' y' not worth wastin' breath on, come
ahead, let's go, lads.

Mrs Crackers: I'll see your parents, don't you worry!

Mr Crackers: [*To* **Scully**] I'll see your father for a start –
even if I have to pick him out of the gutter first.

[**Scully** *goes for him.* **Mrs Crackers** *pulls him back.* **Mad
Dog** *and* **Snotty Dog** *pull* **Scully** *away as* **Mr and Mrs
Crackers** *leer at him. But they move away.*

Another **woman** *with a delinquent eight-year-old*
daughter *and what looks suspiciously like the Dogs' pram,
is advancing behind them*]

Woman: All right, which one of you lot is Snotty Dog O'Gorman? Come on!

Scully: [*To the* **Crackers**] You've had it, you have.

Snotty Dog: Er no missus, listen – it was only a lend – I –

Mrs Crackers: Truth hurt does it, Scully?

[*The* **woman** *pushes the pram at* **Snotty Dog,** *knocking him through the privets*]

Woman: And give us the money back. Now! You can't sell babies.

Mooey: Yisssss, this is excitin'.

Mrs Crackers: And get out of my privets!

[*She slams the door, leaving* **Mr Crackers** *outside. He keeps knocking, trying to be casual as the scene goes on, and* **Snotty Dog** *hands over two one pound notes to the* **woman**]

Little Girl: But mam, mam – he's mine now, I've given him another name –

Woman: Yeah great – Rebecca's a smart name for a baby boy.

Girl: I hate boys. I wanna little girl.

[*She gets dragged off*]

Woman: [*As they go*] I'm warnin' you, madam, when your father gets home . . .

Girl: But I wanna baby, everyone else's got one, I wanna baby . . .

Woman: You'll have to wait until you're sixteen . . .

Snotty Dog: [*Looking around*] Worth a try. I mean, two quid an' three hours o' peace, I don't get many offers like that. [*He looks at the* **girl** *going off*] She said she was a registered child-minder, but small for her age . . .

[*The boys start walking away*]

Mad Dog: [*As they go*] But what're we gonna do now?

Scully: [*Looking back, still angry*] We're goin' back there. To her house, later. [*They look at him*] When they're out.

Mad Dog: Y' mean . . . do a . . . robbery?

Scully: Y' said y' wanted to do something big, Mad Dog. Here's y' chance. Anyway, it won't be a robbery – just gettin' back what's rightfully ours. [*With meaning*] As well as gettin' our own back. Which's what really counts.

Mad Dog: But er, they're still in the house, they might notice, like, an' er, who knows when they'll come out tonight. You know.

Scully: Half past nine, Mad Dog, regular as clockwork, down the British Legion, salute the Queen, two glasses of shandy, a quick game of bingo, and a chorus of 'There'll Always Be An England' [*He looks at* **Mad Dog**] We'll have an hour. Plenty of time.

Mooey: Er, it sounds a bit too excitin' for me. I'll wait for tomorrow.

Mad Dog: But Crackers'll know it's us. She'll report us.

Scully: No she won't. That's what I like about it. [*He smiles at last*]

Mad Dog: Why not? Why won't Crackers report us?

Scully: Can y' imagine her goin' the police station, walkin' up to Isaiah or one of them, sayin', 'Er excuse me, officer, I'd like to report the robbery of ninety-three second-hand balls'? . . . It's perfect. And it's just what you want. [**Mad Dog** *looks at him*]

Mad Dog: Something big. [*He tries to rise to his full height, and looks around nervously*] Er, all right . . . but does it have to be tonight?

Mooey: Er yeah, 'cos Scull's takin' me an' M –

Scully: [*Hissing at him*] Not now, Mooey!

Mooey: Er yeah, I know, it's tomorrow night, half past seven outside the 'Bow an' Arrow'. I can't wait. Neither can our Marie. She might even have a bath, she said so. [**Scully** *stares at him*]

Mad Dog: Y' not are y', Scull? Marie Morgan? *Marie Morgan!*

Scully: Nah! Course I'm not.

Mooey: [*As we fade, quietly to* **Mad Dog**] He is y' know, Mad Dog. He's just shy . . . but our Marie isn't though . . .

10   Outside the Leighs' house

It is night. The 'gang' is approaching the Leighs' house through the field at the back of the house. The pram is bouncing about madly.

Scully: Walk up an' down in their road, Snotty Dog, look as if you're tryin' to settle the baby, an' act as lookout. Go 'head, Mad Dog, get goin'.

[**Mad Dog** *starts climbing over fences*]

Mad Dog: I think I can hear their telly. Are you sure they're –

Scully: They leave that on as well. [*Urgently*] Come on, will y'!

[**Scully** *pushes him off the fence*]

11   The front of the house

In the darkness, we see **Snotty Dog** *parading up and down the road, rocking the pram and saying such novelties as 'coochie-coo'.*

12   The back of the house

We see **Mad Dog** *testing the drainpipe, hoping that it is loose. We see the bathroom window and the tight squeeze that* **Mad Dog** *has to get through it. Then we see* **Scully** *and* **Mooey** *waiting at the back kitchen door. After a while the door opens.* **Mad Dog** *has a portable television in one hand. He holds it up like the F.A. Cup and slobbers with excitement.*

Mad Dog: I seen it first, it's mine, I bagsed it! An' y' wanna see –

Scully: I told y' – no robbin' – we're not takin' hostages – just releasing prisoners. Let's go an' find them.

13   Inside the house

Scully *walks towards the hall, but* **Mooey** *is drawn towards the fridge. He opens it.*

Mooey: [*Hopefully*] Yis ... double yis ... food.

[*We see* **Scully** *and* **Mad Dog** *whipping through the rooms in the house, looking for balls – to no avail.* **Scully** *can't understand. They walk back into the back kitchen.*

They see **Mooey** *(having destroyed bread, cheese, ham and tomatoes in an attempt at sandwiches) has cut himself opening a tin of fruit. He is standing there with blood dropping onto the pineapple chunks.* **Scully** *takes him to the sink and pours cold water on the cut*]

Mooey: Er, can I have a plaster, Scull – an' er one to take home as well.

Scully: Look in the bathroom Mad Dog.

[**Mad Dog** *goes to the downstairs bathroom door and opens it. Balls of all shapes, sizes, colours and age descend around him like boulders in an avalanche, hundreds and hundreds and hundreds bouncing and rolling into the back kitchen. When the storm settles,* **Mad Dog**, **Mooey** *and* **Scully** *peep into the bathroom. In the bath are the oldest balls of all*]

Scully: [*Looking at one of the balls and reading*] 'The Stanley Matthews Special' . . .

Mad Dog: [*With distaste*] Y' know what that means, don't y' . . . all the balls in there . . .

Scully: I know. It means that those two never have a –

[*There is a firm knock on the door.* **Mooey** *jumps, yelps and turns, soaking his sleeve in the water from the tap.* **Mad Dog** *heads frantically for the door, falling spectacularly over nearly every ball in the back kitchen*]

Scully: Calm down – it won't be them, will it? They wouldn't knock on their own front door, would they?

[**Snotty Dog** *comes racing through the back kitchen with the pram and crying baby. He starts talking, then looks at all the balls*]

Snotty Dog: It's a feller. Two fellers in a big . . . car.

Mad Dog: Oh hey, the Law. Me mam'll kill me.

Scully: Does it look like the Law?

Snotty Dog: [*Part near hysterical, part fascinated with the balls*] Er no, it's . . . er . . . their car's fallin' apart an' one of them's got long hair. But they've been up an' down twice. I watched them . . . Were all these in –

[*The door goes again – they all jump*]

Scully: Hey though, I bet they're on the rob as well.

Mad Dog: This is no time f' jokes, Scull. We're trapped in here, well, we might be, they could have us surrounded already. Come on, what're we gonna do?

Mooey: Er, I'm goin' to plead insanity.

Mad Dog: Yeah, it's all right f'you, you've got the qualifications – but what about us?

Scully: Stay there – just stay there. An' don't move!

[**Scully** *goes towards the front door, and switches the hall light out. The knocker goes again just as he does so. We hear three half-strangled yelps.* **Scully** *goes to the door*]

Mad Dog: [*Faintly*] If it's the paperboy, I'll kick his brains in . . .

[**Scully** *opens the door, slightly. He sees* **Dalglish** *standing there. He slams the door shut, then opens it again. A* **man** *of about thirty-five stands there, just a little shifty and shabby*]

Man: I'm lookin' for an old friend of mine, son, John Hunter and his missus. They haven't moved have they? I could have sworn they lived here – got a daughter about the same age as you. Fourteen or so she'll be.

Scully: I'm nearly seventeen, pal.

Man: The daughter's name was er, Janet.

Scully: Got blonde hair – sometimes wears pigtails?

Man: Yes, now y' come to mention it, I think she used to.

Scully: Wears glasses and a brace on her top teeth?

Man: [*Trying to be surprised*] By God y' exactly right. Y' do know her.

Scully: Sorry feller, never seen anyone around here that looks like that.

[**Scully** *turns to us. We see the fastest of flashes of the cartoon stereotype of a robber, with eye mask, and a bag of 'swag' on his shoulder. We come back to* **Scully.** *He grins at us, and looks beyond the* **man** *towards the car and the roadway. He stops grinning, and walks out a pace onto the front step as the* **man** *talks on. We just catch sight of* **Mrs Scully** *going across the corner of the road, caught in a car's headlights, with the man at her side hidden in her shadow*]

Man: Er yes, well, I'm sure they used t' live in this road. Still never mind, I'll try the next one up.

[*We see the* **man** *now staring at* **Scully,** *who finally looks at him*]

Scully: Yeah, you do that.

[*The* **man** *walks away.* **Scully** *retreats to the shadows, turns around, and sees* **Mad Dog, Snotty Dog** *and* **Mooey** *peeping around the back kitchen door at different heights. Grinning,* **Scully** *looks back to the* **man** *as he starts to walk across the road to his car*]

Scully: Hey! [*The* **man** *stops, and turns slowly*] D' y' mind shuttin' the gate after y'?

[*We see the field just behind the* **Leighs'** *back garden, in near darkness, as ball after ball after ball is thrown and kicked high on to the field.*

We come back to **Scully** *and the others on the back door step. The portable television is on the kitchen table*]

Scully: Listen, Mad Dog, what d' y' want with a picture of a green girl an' three plaster ducks? We didn't come to strip the joint. All we wanted was the balls. That's what's so good about it.

Mad Dog: Y' kiddin'. Leave my portable telly behind?

Snotty Dog: We won't take that much.

Mad Dog: She won't hardly notice ... Not really.

Mooey: Can I take the rest of the spam?

Scully: Y' stupid gets – can't y' see – Crackers won't dare report the loss of a bathroom full of balls – but she'll be scratchin' at the soddin' ceilin' if half her house's gone with them.

[*There is pause.* **Scully** *picks a couple of balls up. The others do the same. Three go on the pram.* **Mad Dog** *looks at the telly again*]

Mad Dog: I suppose so. [*They go out,* **Mad Dog** *banging the door, and walk down the garden*] ... We'd better go the long way home.

14   The park

We see them walking along a path in the park, by the housing estate. **Mooey** *is looking forward to tomorrow now.*

Mooey: Is it Southport, Scull ... Or the fair at New Brighton? Hey, is it? They're excitin', er, so I've been told ...

Scully: Look Moo, there's somethin' you'd better know right now – me an' –

[*We hear laughter and drunken shouting coming from the main road. It is a hill, with a zebra crossing near the park path. We see* **Scully** *and the others approach the crowd by the zebra, trying to see what they are laughing at. They move around the edge till there is a space. Their backs are turned* *to the steep brow. They see the cause of the laughter. It is* **Mr Scully** *lying flat out in front of the zebra crossing with* **Mr O'Gorman**, *both totally legless, trying to 'play' the zebra like a piano, and singing 'Ebony and Ivory']*

Mr Scully and Mr O'Gorman: [*Together*] 'Ebony and ivory, together in perfect harmony . . .'

Mr Scully: Hey! These piano keys're big . . .

[*As the boys watch in abject silence, they see* **Mr and Mrs Leigh** *approaching, looking eagerly to see what is going on*]

Scully: Drop them!

[*A girl in the crowd looks around, shocked.* **Scully** *lets go the balls he is carrying. They bounce back behind him down the hill. The others comply, and we see eleven balls of various sizes being dropped behind the boys, bounce down the road, finally past a puzzled bus queue. As* **Mr and Mrs Leigh** *realize who the two men are, they focus on the* **Dogs** *and* **Scully**. *We see a sneer of victory on* **Mrs Leigh's** *face directed at the boys. Each returns the sneer with hatred, except* **Mooey**, *who thinks she is smiling strangely and imitates her sneer. We see* **Snotty Dog** *as* **Mad Dog** *whispers to him. The whisper sinks in. They glance at* **Scully**. *They go to say something, but* **Scully** *is forging through the crowd.* **Mooey** *goes to go with him, but is yanked back by the others. We see* **Scully** *picking his father up, as the others slink back the way they came*]

15   Outside Scully's house

We see **Scully** *entering his pathway, past an* **elderly gent** *at the gate muttering something about it being his turn. We hear* *sounds of bronchial passion from the front step. His* **Gran** *and the* **other elderly gent** *are suitably entwined by the front door.* **Scully** *ignores them as he puts the key in the door. He goes in.*

16   Inside Scully's house

Gran: If you're makin' a cup of tea, Francis . . .

[**Scully** *moves into the house. As he does so, we hear the back kitchen door leading into the back garden being opened and rapidly shut.* **Scully** *heads for the back kitchen. He opens the door leading to the back kitchen, and sees* **Mrs Scully** *at the door that had just been shut. There is a sense of disorder about her*]

Scully: Who was that?

Mrs Scully: Who was what? [*He looks at her*] The door? It was me. I thought I heard something outside. That's all.

Scully: [*Going to the door and opening it*] I saw you tonight.

Mrs Scully: Oh aye? [*She turns away, and busies herself making a pot of tea*] And?

Scully: And then I saw me dad, but he didn't see me. There again, neither did you.

Mrs Scully: Is all this supposed to mean something?

Scully: Who were you with?

Mrs Scully: Does it matter?

Scully: Yeah. It does to me.

Mrs Scully: Well, it doesn't to me. [*Pause*] D'you know how old I am? [*He shrugs*] I'm forty-six years old, Francis.

Scully: Yeah – so?

Mrs Scully: So you're a long time dead. All y' dreams 're kicked from under you by my age. [*Pause*] Mine are anyway. Y' just get through it all the best y' can. Now if you've got anything to say, say it now. Otherwise, get to bed.

Scully: [*Long pause*] I've still got me dreams, Mam. Some'd say they were soft dreams . . . there's even people in the dreams, people I feel I can reach out and touch . . . [*Shakes his head*] . . . and other people've got their dreams for me as well.

Mrs Scully: [*Lightly*] Aren't you the lucky one?

Scully: But their dreams are even softer than mine.

Mrs Scully: No dreams are soft, Francis. And God knows, y' lucky that other people care enough to have dreams for y'. [*Approaches him*] Y'father was in my dreams. I cared for y'father. [*Misses a beat*] But now he's past caring for himself. Keep y'dreams as long as y'can, son, there's nothin' else to keep around here. An' don't dismiss those dreams that other people have for you. Y'never know, they might be right. [**Scully** *turns away*] And don't worry – I was Rita Hayworth once. In my dreams.

Scully: Yeah – an' me dad was Clark Gable.

Mrs Scully: Actually, he thought he was Errol Flynn.

Scully: [*At the door*] Me gran wants a cup of tea, an' vaseline f'her love bites . . . [*Going to the back kitchen door*] See y' later . . .

Mrs Scully: Where y' going?

Scully: See a dreamer I should have seen earlier.

17   A road

We see **Scully** *walking down a road. It is raining heavily. He hears police sirens, and sees the police car, and the mere flash* *of* **Isaiah's** *face at the window as it speeds past.* **Scully** *turns a corner and goes. We see* **Mad Dog, Mooey, Snotty Dog** *and pram appear from an alleyway, peeping around the corner, trying to be surreptitious.* **Snotty Dog** *has the portable television on the pram and* **Mooey** *drops one of the three ducks, while* **Mad Dog** *hits him with the painting.*

18   A middle-class estate

We follow **Scully** *through a road of a middle-class estate, soaked to the skin, and down a path to the door of a house. He knocks on the door and waits. The lights go on after a time. Then a figure comes down the stairs and goes to the front door. We can see* **Steve** *in a dressing gown, still half asleep as he opens up.* **Scully** *goes to say something, then just shrugs his shoulders and stands there. He looks at* **Steve** *and smiles and nods his head.* **Steve** *grins at him, hugely.*

We freeze the frame on **Steve's** *grin, but somewhere in the far distance a police siren goes again.*

Episode 6

Scully's big night out with Marie Morgan (Gilly Coman) on Otterspool promenade

Episode 6

---

1 A road

*We see **Scully** walking to school the next day. We see he is smiling. Then we see why he is smiling. Every kid going into school with him has a ball of some shape or description.*

2 A classroom

*We see **Scully** in a lesson. The **teacher** is a big man who at least keeps them quiet. A messenger comes, disturbing the dozing. The teacher looks at the message. He grins to himself and bangs the blackboard duster for attention.*

Teacher: All right, pay attention now, an important message from Mrs Heath about the school pantomime. [*Over-the-top yawns are heard.* **Scully** *puts his desk lid up*] There's a meeting in the hall now for all those who are performing in Cinderella. [*Misses a beat, looks down at the message*] That's you, Scully –

[*For a very few seconds, we hear guffaws, raspberries and expressions of disbelief.* **Scully** *glares at them, particularly at* **Kelly***, who waves, flop-wristed at him. It is all stopped dead as the* **teacher** *adds* –

Teacher: . . . and you Bignall.

[*There is silence as* **Bignall** *looks around meaningfully. He joins* **Scully**]

Scully: [*Surprised*] What are you doing in it?

Bignall: [*As they leave the class*] I'm one of the broker's men – and I'm the head bouncer on the door before the show starts . . .

3   The school hall

We see the school hall. **Mrs Heath** *is at the front, sitting on the assembly stage, lighting an inevitable Capstan Full Strength.* **Steve** *is sitting at the side of the stage. Facing them are about forty kids, of both sexes, ages ranging from eleven to sixteen. Sitting deliberately at the back, away from everyone else, are* **Joanna**, *and* **Scully** *with* **Bignall**. **Mrs Heath** *smiles at them, and focuses on* **Scully** *for a second.*

Mrs Heath: Now then the two ugly sisters are going to be Maureen Connor and Janet Fraser.

[*We see a flash of disappointment from both girls at not being Cinderella, but then, like runners-up in a beauty contest, they pretend to be thrilled.* **Scully** *watches them*]

Scully: [*To* **Bignall**] Well, they won't need no make-up.

[**Bignall** *grins*]

Mrs Heath: Baron Hardup is Harold Fowler who was so good last year as the Woodcutter in Red Riding Hood.

Scully: Apart from losing three fingers an' droppin' his axe on his toes all the time. Look at him, y'd think he'd been nominated f'an Oscar . . .

Mrs Heath: Cinderella, and it was a close race between three or four girls, but Cinderella goes to Joanna Kew. [*Dagger-like looks shoot at her from every girl in the group.*

Joanna *looks delighted and surprised, amid the odd mutterings of 'But she's black']* Yes, and for those of you who feel it's important to distinguish between black and white, in our version, Cinderella is the adopted sister of those two ugly old monsters over there. *[She smiles at the two girls who are glaring at* **Joanna***]*

Maureen: *[Like a ventriloquist]* She's dead at playtime . . .

Mrs Heath: Now then, the handsome prince. A *very* difficult decision again, and very much a late decision. *[We focus on* **Scully** *preening quietly. He nudges* **Bignall,** *who looks at him slightly disbelievingly]* This character has to be good-looking, debonair, able to dance, suave, pleasant and charming. *[***Scully** *nods to all of those, except the dancing: he recognizes himself]* We really have to believe that he could simply sweep Cinderella off her feet. *[***Scully** *nudges* **Bignall** *again]* And with that in mind, I've decided on Tony Morris.

*[***Scully** *is about to lean back and take the stares. He double takes in disbelief, and we see* **Tony Morris,** *a blandly attractive normal fifth form boy, who smiles nervously.* **Mrs Heath** *continues]*

Scully: Well, I didn't think it'd be him. He's the last one I would have picked. Just 'cos he can dance, that's all it is.

Mrs Heath: *[Underneath* **Scully's** *sourness for a time]* The footmen are John Sloan and Paddy Lewis, the father is Kevin Donovan, the King is Tony Coates, and the Queen is Lillian Kelly . . . *[She looks up]* Scully. *[Quite a few others turn round]* I think you've got the hardest part, but I also think it's the best one.

Scully: I know. The silver slipper.

Mrs Heath: No. *[She stamps her cigarette out]* The Fairy Godmother.

[*Laughter*]

Scully: [*Standing*] Wha'? *Wha'*? I'm not bein' seen in no shawl an' high heels – not to mention the magic wand and the pointed hat. That's not what I had in mind at all.

Mrs Heath: What part was it that you wanted, then?

Scully: Well, I thought I was going to be the Prince. [*Lots of laughter*] Well I did.

Steve: Take it easy Scull, early days yet.

Scully: But I'm not dressin' up as no woman, so that's that. I'd have to emigrate. [*Looking around*] Hey Fowler, will you stop laughin'!

Mrs Heath: Just go through the script and look at the lines for now. We'll rehearse at four o'clock this afternoon. And don't worry.

[*The others go up for their scripts.* **Scully** *sits stubbornly by* **Bignall** *and looks around. The bell goes for the end of the lesson*]

Scully: It's true though, I would've been the Prince if I could dance. All the other bits were me. [*He looks angrily at* **Tony Morris** *as he walks back with his script*] I'm going to learn all your lines, Morris, and then I'm going to break y' legs just before the first night.

Bignall: [*Standing*] Come 'head, Mother, let's get our script.

[*They approach* **Steve** *and* **Mrs Heath. Joanna** *is collecting a script*]

Scully: You'd better be home for midnight, I'm warnin' y'.

Joanna: [*As she walks away*] So had you, from what I hear . . .

[*As* **Scully** *looks at her, the hall door opens. We see* **Kelly**,

Mad Dog *and a couple more at the door, looking in.* **Kelly** *talks to one of the kids going out with their script. There is a sudden burst of laughter from the gang]*

Kelly: *[Waving at* **Scully***]* Hallo Sweety! *[To* **Mrs Heath***]* I want two tickets f' the front row, Miss – I wanna see his knickers!

Mrs Heath: Go and squeeze your pimples, you useless slimy little boy!

Kelly: *[Quietly as the others snigger]* Yes miss. *[He ducks out]*

Scully: See what I mean though. This is just the start. I'm goin' to have more fights over this than . . .

Steve: Francis. *[Motions for* **Scully** *to move away with him.* **Scully** *reluctantly follows]* Thank you.

Scully: Think nothin' of it – I don't . . . Y' could've told me.

Steve: I worked on the principle that what you didn't know . . .

Scully: Till I found out.

Steve: And then it'd be too late.

*[***Scully** *looks out of the hall window, and sees* **Kelly** *grotesquely kissing the window.* **Scully** *makes a move for the window.* **Steve** *stops him]*

Scully: It isn't too late. *[***Scully** *gives* **Steve** *the script back]*

Steve: Yes it is. You see, I've already kept my side of the bargain – I've got you a trial game with Liverpool after school tomorrow.

*[***Scully** *looks at him very carefully, and hesitates]*

Scully: *Tomorrow* night?

Steve: Four-thirty at the training ground.

Scully: That was quick.

Steve: I used to be a player myself. [**Scully** *nods*] Well, if an old player can't take advantage of the one or two contacts he's still got in the game, who can?

Scully: Er but I'm not fit, Steve. I haven't trained. Me boots 're too small. Y'know I didn't expect – so fast. I'm not makin' excuses.

Steve: You might not need any. We'll see . . . This *is* what you wanted, isn't it?

Scully: [*Taking the script back*] Yeah. I wanted it all right. But tomorrow . . .

Steve: Better this way, no time to worry and sweat over it. And then you'll have it over with. And then you might know. And the quicker you know the better.

Scully: Just one more thing Steve . . . What're y' doin' all this for?

[**Steve** *looks at him for some seconds, then digs into the inside pocket of his jacket. He takes out a wallet, and takes a picture out of the wallet. He gives it to* **Scully**, *who looks at the picture, not understanding*]

Scully: [*After a pause*] They your kids Steve?

Steve: Right. [*He takes the picture back*]

Scully: Yeah, great . . . but, er . . . I don't understand.

Steve: [*Quietly*] Three daughters.

Mrs Heath: [*Shouting after him*] Don't forget Francis, four o'clock . . .

4 The school toilets

We see **Scully** *in a cubicle of a school toilet, fully clothed. He is reading the script, and wincing. He leans back.*

Scully: [*To himself*] 'I have watched over you from afar, my little darling, Cinders' ... 'my little darling Cinders' ... Ohhh, I can see them now ... [*Mimicking* **Kelly**] 'Get em off, Scull!' ... 'What're y' doin' after the show, honey ...' [*He holds his head in his hands, and hears the voices of some kids entering. He recognizes* **Mad Dog**'*s voice, and listens*]

Mad Dog: But hey, no listen, this is aces this bit, even though I do say so meself, but right, we're there with all the balls – oh an' hey – don't say anythin' to Scull about this – he was dead jealous it was me, an' I don't want to upset him – but we're there in the back kitchen, I'm like organizin' gettin' the balls out of the iron bath, when there's a knock on the front door – well naturally, the others' bottle went straight off – an' they were all for divin' out the back, but not me, nah – I took charge, didn't I – calmed everyone down – an' strolled through the hall – opened the door – an' then – an' then – guess what boys –

Scully: There was this voice from out the toilet, sayin' you were a rotten stinkin' liar, Mad Dog.

[*There is a pause.* **Scully** *opens the toilet door, and faces* **Mad Dog**]

Mad Dog: Er, hallo, Scull. I er, didn't know you were there ...

Scully: Go on, Mad Dog, you were at the door ... I was in the kitchen bein' scared ...

Mad Dog: [*Sulking*] ... Well, I er, sort of ... it didn't quite happen like that. Actually, it was Scully at the door ... not me. [*He looks away. The others grin and drift out. When they are gone,* **Mad Dog** *looks angrily at* **Scully**] Why did y' do that?

Scully: [*Half laughing*] Why did you tell them it was you at the door?

Mad Dog: 'Cos it was my big moment. I'd done something big.

Scully: But you didn't do it – I did.

Mad Dog: I wanted to tell them somethin' big I'd done, but I couldn't . . .

Scully: Why not?

Mad Dog: 'Cos I couldn't. [*He won't look at him*]

Scully: What was it?

Mad Dog: Nothin' . . . [*Starting to go*] I still think it was sly, doin' that to me . . .

Scully: Oh come on, Mad Dog, y' can tell everyone it was you. I don't care.

Mad Dog: It's too late now . . .

5   The school hall

We see the school hall after school. It is the first rehearsal. This, to a degree, can be improvised, but the basis should be as follows.

In the background, on stage, we see the ugly sisters and Cinderella, scripts in hand, walking through the part of the play where the ugly sisters are about to go to the ball, and are leaving, laughing at Cinderella, left to brush up.

In the foreground, we see **Scully** *walking up and down, side stage, holding the script and muttering to himself. He hears his entrance lines and turns and waits.*

Joanna: (*as* **Cinderella**) Oh I am so sad. I so much wanted to go to the ball. It seems at times as if I haven't got a friend in the world.

[**Scully** *bounces on. The giggles start*]

Joanna: (*as* **Cinderella**) Oh my goodness! Who are you?

Scully: (*as* **Fairy Godmother**) I am your fairy godmother. Do not be afraid. Dry your eyes my dear, and tell me why you are feeling so sad, because if I can, I will help you. That is what fairy godmothers are for.

[*He pats her on the back, and knocks her forward a few yards. The giggles turn to laughter. He looks up, then looks back at the script. He doesn't understand why they are laughing. As* **Cinderella** *tells her story, trying not to corpse, and succeeding for most of the time,* **Scully** *acts like an old woman, arms folded, mouthing the words, looking absurdly sad, shaking his head*]

Joanna: (*as* **Cinderella**) You see, Fairy Godmother, my two terrible stepsisters hate me very much, and they always tell lies about me, and they are so clever that my father believes them instead of me. They beat me and pinch me and laugh at me. And tonight . . . tonight . . . they've . . . they've gone off to the ball to meet the Prince . . . and they won't let me go with them.

[*At this point, she is supposed to break down, and* **Scully** *goes down on one knee and puts his arm around her. But* **Joanna** *breaks into hysterics instead, and so do the rest of the company.* **Mrs Heath** *starts choking on her cigarette smoke, and* **Steve** *has to turn away, almost doubled up.* **Scully** *looks around, bewildered*]

Mrs Heath: [*Finally*] Start again, please, Francis. From your entrance.

[**Scully** *doesn't think much of the idea, but goes back.* **Joanna** *feeds him his entrance line again*]

Joanna: (*as* **Cinderella**). . . it seems at times as if I haven't got a friend in the world.

[**Scully** *bounces in again. The giggles start again*]

Joanna: (*as* **Cinderella**) Oh my goodness – who are you?

Scully: (*as* **Fairy Godmother**)I am your fairy godmother. Be afraid – er no, don't be!

[*Everyone dissolves again, except* **Scully**. **Joanna** *runs off stage.* **Scully** *throws his script down*]

Scully: Friggin' hell! It was only a little mistake – it's not that funny. I don't know what you're all laughin' at me for.

Mrs Heath: We're not laughing *at* you, Scully. We're laughing *with* you.

Scully: But I'm not doin' nothin', I'm just sayin' what's written down here. And there's not one joke in it.

Mrs Heath: But it's as if you've studied someone doing just those things.

Scully: I was thinkin' of me gran. Can I bring a bottle of gin an' two sex-starved pensioners on with me? Hey, I've gorra crackin' idea, Mrs Heath. No, listen – instead of me bein' Old Mary godmother, why couldn't I be a godfather y' know, like in the Mafia. Hey? [*There is no answer*] (*As Humphrey Bogart:*) OK sweetheart, don't be scared pussycat, I'm your godfather, now who's doing the dirty on you, brown eyes? [*He stops and looks around*]

Mrs Heath: It's very good, but I don't think the juniors and the infants would understand.

Scully: I don't care about them. What about me mates? What about our road when they come? They're not goin' to understand neither if they see me wearin' make-up an' lippy, with two coconuts strapped to me chest [*He looks at her*] Yeah all right . . . [*He walks to the wings to wait, and stands there. He looks at us*] I know one thing – Kenny Dalglish wouldn't do this.

[*We see* **Dalglish** *at his side, dressed like a fairy godmother*]

Dalglish: Who wouldn't?

[*As* **Scully** *stares at him,* **Dalglish** *bounces on stage*]

Dalglish: I am your fairy godmother, do not be afraid!

6   A housing estate

We see **Scully** *walking through the estate, on the way home. He goes through an area surrounded by high-rise flats, head down, miles away. We hear someone shouting: not clear, distanced, and disguised, perhaps high-pitched. 'Scully' is part of the shout. He glances up but keeps walking. Then we hear another voice. We hear 'Marie' this time.* **Scully** *stops and looks up at all the flats, but doesn't know which block it's coming from. For the first time, we hear clearly:*

1st Voice: We know where y' goin', we know where y' goin . . .

2nd Voice: All right Scull! Goin' t' see y' girlfriend, Marie Morgan?

3rd Voice: The school bike!

1st Voice: The bin-man's moll!

2nd Voice: Give her one for me!

3rd Voice: I've already given her one!

1st Voice: So's everyone else!

2nd Voice: Except Scully!

[*Laughter from all three, hidden away.*

Scully *swirls around at first, trying to identify where the voices are coming from, but cannot work it out. As they continue, he puts his head down again, begins to walk away, faster and faster till he is running . . . while the voices seem to run with him*]

7   Mooey's road

We see **Scully** *still running. He reaches* **Mooey's** *road, stops running, and tries to gather his breath. He approaches the front door of* **Mooey's** *house. Inevitably,* **Marie** *is there, somewhat over-dressed, as usual.*

Scully: [*Quickly*] Er listen Marie, I've just remembered, I don't know how I forgot really but –

Marie: Y' can't come out tonight.

Scully: [*With slight surprise*] Er yeah. I'm really –

Marie: But you can. And you are.

Scully: No, y'see –

Marie: 'Cos if you don't, I'll make you the laughin' stock of Liverpool.

Scully: [*Glancing around*] I'm beginning to think I already am. Look –

Marie: I've heard them as well, I've heard them for years – little boys. And I was beginning to think you were a man. I'll have to tell everyone differently now, won't I? [*She smiles sweetly at him*] And then there's the robbery . . .

Scully: What robbery?

Marie: The one you and the Dogs and my soft brother did last night. You wouldn't want that spread around, would you? Honeybunch.

Scully: It wasn't a robbery – but that's blackmail.

Marie: I know. I think it must be because I love you so much. [*She grins*]

Scully: But you don't want to go out with me, Marie. I haven't started shavin' yet, me breath smells, I've got pimples in unexpected places, I'm a fairy in the school play, I don't know nothin' neither – y' know ... about girls ...

Marie: That's why I want to go out with you. I'll show you, Francis. I'll give you a good time ... [*She pouts*]

Scully: Er well, er if y' put it like that.

Marie: Outside the 'Bow and Arrow', don't be late. [*She goes to turn away*]

Scully: But there'll be a lot of people around and like –

Marie: I know.

[*As she turns away,* **Mooey** *bounds to the door*]

Mooey: Yis! It's not half seven already is it? Smart, I'll just get me coat –

[*As he turns away,* **Marie** *drags him back by the neck into the house.* **Scully** *turns towards the pavement defeated, and* **Joanna** *walks past the house, carrying her script. She looks at him, unsmiling*]

8   Scully's house

We see **Scully** *entering his house. Inevitably, at the gate are the* **two elderly gents. Scully** *closes the door and enters the living room – but not for long. He stands at the doorway and sees* **Gran** *standing in front of* **Henry,** *slightly unsteady. As* **Henry** *sits listening to his train noises, she is trying to talk to him.* **Arthur** *is reading the* Judy *annual while* **Mrs Barrett**

and **Tony** *don't seem to have moved from the previous episode.*
Rita *is standing above* **Tony** *like a volcano.*

Gran: D' you know what, Henry . . . Henry, once y' could get
the train from Liverpool to Llandudno, Henry, for one and
eightpence ha'penny, one and eightpence ha'penny return,
not single, a single'd be . . .

Rita: Tony, I said I'm going.

Gran: It'd be half of one and eightpence ha'penny . . .

Rita: Tony Scully, I won't say it again.

Gran: I'm trying to talk to you Henry. About trains, trains,
Henry . . . Henry.

Rita: I'm going Tony.

Gran: Oh you stupid gormless get, I don't know why I
bother.

Rita: [*Erupting out*] Goodbye, Tony. Goodbye forever!

[*As* **Rita** *bangs out of the house,* **Scully** *goes into the back
kitchen*]

9   Scully's kitchen

Mrs Scully *is sitting down, having a cigarette and a cup of
tea.*

Scully: Can you lend me a couple of quid, Mam?

Mrs Scully: I haven't got it, son, honestly. Not till pay-day
tomorrow.

Scully: It's all right. Has Tony got anything?

Mrs Scully: Have y' looked at him the last couple of days?
He hasn't got any life, never mind money. I asked him
before if there'd been a death in the family – an' Florrie
Barrett started cryin'.

Scully: Are you going out tonight?

Mrs Scully: I told y', I haven't got a penny. Bus fare to work, that's all.

Scully: I thought maybe someone might take you out. [*He looks at her*]

Mrs Scully: And what if they are? . . . I'll probably go over to the Labour Club after. If Florrie comes out of her coma.

[**Scully** *crosses towards the hall door*]

Mrs Scully: [*Lightly*] Have a good time tonight. With Marie.

[**Scully** *jerks around, she grins at him*]

Scully: Arrgh! Who told you?

Mrs Scully: I think I read it in the *Daily Mirror.*

Scully: Crikey Bill. I can't keep anythin' a secret. An' I'm not, y' know 'goin' out' with her, Mam. What's more, Mooey's probably comin' with us. Don't look like that – he's got his heart set on it. But Marie, she's . . . y' must have heard what they say about her.

Mrs Scully: It's not what people say, son, or what's said about them – it's what they do. I don't give a monkey's wrench what people say about me. Marie Morgan's probably exactly the same. [*She stands up to make the tea*] I knew her mother, Maureen – rough, but a lovely girl . . . till she went mad. [**Scully** *goes to go out again*] Nevertheless, remember what I always say to Tony – 'Be careful or buy a pram.' [*She drags the bag of potatoes out from under the sink with a sigh.* **Scully** *again makes a move*] Oh and by the way, Mrs Bignall said you could borrow Brian's boots for your trial tomorrow . . .

[**Scully** *has almost gone out of the room. He leans back in and stares at his mother. She laughs as we fade*]

10   The stairs

We see **Scully** *at the top of the stairs looking down, listening for a second.*

Gran: [*Out of sight*] Florrie . . . Florrie, y' don't fancy a blind date, do y' – makin' up a foursome . . . you can choose which one y' want . . . all y' have to do is look out of the window . . . Florrie, what're y' cryin' for . . .? Will *no one* talk to me in this house?

[**Scully** *goes to* **Tony's** *room. He dashes in, and dashes out with a large tin of talc, aftershave, a shirt and a packet of cigarettes. He goes into his own room and locks the door*]

11   Scully's bedroom

We see **Scully** *in his bedroom, a room full of* **Scully's** *Liverpool F.C. and Dalglish pictures, plus* **Arthur's** *posters on etiquette and make-up.* **Scully** *is in his underpants, facing the mirror, studying his body doubtfully.*

Scully: [*With an American accent*] Marie . . . Marie . . . the first time I looked into those deep blue eyes of yours . . . [*His own voice*] I didn't know whether you were lookin' at me or someone to the left of me . . . but that's the way you are, Marie . . . crosseyed . . . [*He takes his trousers from between the mattress and the base of the bed, and puts them on as he talks*] Kenny, if you're there tomorrow – son – watch out – be prepared to be amazed – who knows – soon you might want me to be in your dreams. [*He looks at himself in the mirror*] Pictured today leaving Heathrow Airport for their honeymoon in Hawaii, Francis Scully of Liverpool and England fame, and his beautiful bride, Joanna . . . when asked, Joanna said, 'We first fell in love when Francis was playing the Fairy Godmother in

Cinderella. He just waved his magic wand at me and that was that . . .'

[*He scowls in disbelief, then examines his face closely. He squeezes a pimple, and quietly scrapes it off the mirror. He gets the aftershave and throws it in abundance over his face and under his arms. He unzips his trousers and goes to throw some down his underpants, but just stops in time. He reaches out and takes* **Tony's** *large tin of talc. He shakes it like a sauce bottle, lifts his trousers and underpants away from himself and begins to pour the talc down, studying his face as he does. The lid comes off the talc. We fade as* **Scully** *tries to remove 400 grams of talc from his underpants and trousers*]

12   A pub

We see **Scully** *waiting at the side of the pub in the dark of the evening, hidden as far as possible, but able to watch the bus-stop in the distance.*

Finally, we see **Marie** *walking towards the bus-stop. We see* **Marie** *being followed, a few yards behind, by a very plaintive* **Mooey**, *holding a balloon on a piece of string. Every so often, she turns and gives* **Mooey** *GBH on the ear – to no effect.* **Mooey** *sidles up to her. She moves away. He moves with her. She moves. He moves. She quietly stamps her stilettos into his pumps and twists her heel. She then moves on.* **Mooey** *limps on. They are going sideways along the bus shelter.* **Marie** *rummages in her handbag.* **Mooey** *leans across to watch. She takes a hat pin out and bursts his balloon.* **Mooey** *can't quite believe it, and tries to make his balloon fly again. He looks at* **Marie** *sadly and feels her hat pin.* **Marie** *moves away.* **Mooey** *goes to follow her.* **Marie** *puts her handbag down.* **Mooey** *stops and looks at her. Carefully she rolls up her sleeve. He still watches her.* **Marie** *spits on her right fist.* **Mooey** *is fascinated.*

Marie *drops him with a right to the chin. As* **Mooey** *hurtles backwards, he crashes into the bus shelter.*

Marie *steps casually aside as the shelter disintegrates, picks up her handbag and looks for a bus.* **Mooey** *climbs out of the wreckage, completely unhurt, but he has got the message, and backs away from* **Marie***. He half waves, and bangs into a lamp-post. He retreats facing the right way, occasionally looking around. As he goes out of frame, he is trying to blow the balloon up, and jumps up with it to try to give it impetus.*

Scully *glances around. No one is in sight. He turns the collar up on his jacket, puts his head down, tries to look tough and steps out into the deserted car park. As soon as he walks a few yards, his father comes staggering out of the pub and indirectly towards* **Scully.**

Scully: [*Startled*] Oh! Oh, hallo Dad! How's it going?

Mr Scully: Lend us a pound, son. Go on.

Scully: If I did that, I'd be having a night out on ninepence.

Mr Scully: 'S' OK. 'S' all right. 'S no sweat. She's a nice girl, Marie. I knew her mother . . . [*Sadly*] Have a good time. I did. Once . . .

[*He staggers off, and* **Scully** *looks at him, at* **Marie,** *and around. Still no one else is in sight. He strolls towards* **Marie,** *like 'Cool Hand Luke' and, as he reaches her, winks casually.*

Amongst the debris of the bus shelter, a concrete post still remains standing. He leans against it, 'macho' personified]

Scully: Hi!

[*The post falls down*]

Marie: [*Ignoring it*] Hallo Francis. Am I early?

Scully: Er no, about on time, I would think. [*He looks* *around*] Nothin's built to last these days, is it? [*He looks around*] Nice night. Isn't it?

Marie: Y' mean there's nobody around.

Scully: No! Em, mild for the time of the year. Pleasant . . . [*He casually, without looking, tries for her hand. Once she puts her hand up to her hair, and he misses. The second time, just as he goes for it, she puts her hand in her pocket. He gives up, whistles, stops, and looks down the road*] Oh look, here's the bus! [*He puts his hand out, miles too early.* **Marie** *smiles, knowingly. We see the bus draw up to the bus-stop*]

13   Inside the bus

Scully *steps on before* **Marie** *as fast as he can. He tries to hide his conversation with the one-man* **driver.** *As* **Marie** *stands behind him.*

Scully: Two scholars to Otterspool please. Pal.

Driver: Don't mess about, I'm on the late shift, I'm not in the mood.

Scully: Ah believe me, I always have this problem, I look old f' me age.

Driver: So does y'mother there.

Scully: That's not my mother, don't insult my younger sister.

Driver: Thirty-six pence each. Take it or leave it.

Scully: But –

[*The doors fly open behind them.* **Scully** *gives the* **driver** *a pound and gets the change. He scoops it up and goes upstairs as the bus starts up.* **Marie** *follows after him up the stairs, and as* **Scully** *pops his head up on to the top deck, he meets* *wild ribald cheering, and he sees the collected masses of his own class – with the exception of Bignall and Mad Dog – but particularly* **Kelly.**

Scully *turns frantically, and bumps into* **Marie,** *who keeps going.* **Scully** *turns back, and heads for one of the few seats, at the front of the bus, through the jeering mob. He lets* **Marie** *into the inside position on the seat, and sits down heavily. A cloud of talc spurts up from his trousers.* **Marie** *looks at him, but he is already half-way turned around, and doesn't see the cloud as he points back*]

Kelly: All right, Scull! Good hey! A surprise party. Couldn't miss this.

Scully: What d' y' want on y' headstone, Kelly?

Boy: Ask Marie, she knows all about cemeteries.

[*Laughter*]

Kelly: What's it like, lad? Are y'all excited? Is it love?

Scully: Someone has had it tomorrow. Whoever told y'all.

Kelly: [*Happily*] Better see y' friends then. 'Cos that's who told us. That's what friends're for – t' let you down. Good old Mad Dog.

Scully: A friend in need . . .

Kelly: He should've been here himself, it was all planned. [*He laughs*]

Another boy: Y'll like Otterspool Marie, much better than the cemetery.

Kelly: But Scully won't – 'cos he wishes he was dead!

[*Wild laughter.*

As **Kelly** *repeats his joke,* **Scully** *glances at* **Marie,** *then out of the window. He just catches a glimpse of* **Mooey** *walking along the pavement in front of them as a police car* *pulls up alongside him. We see* **Isaiah** *grabbing hold of* **Mooey** *and dragging him toward the police car.* **Scully** *tries to see what is happening through the side windows, but it is lost. He half stands to look back*]

Kelly: Here – his bottle's gone already!

[**Scully** *sits down again, angrily, amid another cloud of talc. He looks at it, and tries to blow it away. He looks at* **Marie**. *She is staring out of the window. We fade as the gang start singing a topical love song . . .*]

14   Otterspool Promenade

We see **Scully** *and* **Marie** *walking through the trees approaching Otterspool Promenade. They are silent.* **Scully** *again briefly tries to swing his hand so that it catches* **Marie's** *– but misses.*

Scully: I'm er goin' for that trial I was tellin' y' about Marie. With Liverpool. Football Club. Tomorrow.

Marie: Are you looking forward to it?

Scully: Oh aye yeah. Deffo. Big chance.

Marie: Just think, when you're famous, I might be able to tell everyone I knew you once. That we had a date.

Scully: [*Looking at her sharply*] Are you takin' the Michael?

Marie: No. [*She grins*] I won't even tell them you tried to get scholars.

[*They walk a little further and approach the promenade, overlooking a low tide sea of mud, bedspreads, bike frames, rusting ditched vehicles and three-piece suites. On the promenade are the occasional covered seating areas, lamp-posts, a few kids on bikes, a couple of pensioners and the*

odd courting couple.
It is dark, except for the light from the lamp-post]

Scully: [*Desperate for something to say*] It's er, still a nice night. Isn't it? [*She nods*] I er . . . yeah. I hope it's a nice night tomorrow. As well. For me trial. Although it isn't really at night. It's in the afternoon . . . at the training ground. They supply most of the kit. As well . . .

[*They approach a large mattress, lying over the railing of the prom, where someone hasn't been able to get it into the river.* **Scully** *stops in front of it, and looks at it*]

Scully: Hey look at that! [*She looks at it*] See that – see that mattress – well that's the same make as the mattress on my bed!

Marie: Is that a fact?

Scully: [*Getting closer to her*] Yeah. Er, what does a mattress make you think of, Marie?

Marie: Sleep.

[*We see* **Scully** *looking crestfallen as* **Marie** *walks away. We also see that she is smiling to herself. She is teasing him on gently and enjoying every minute. He catches her up.*
They sit down in a covered area, by a lamp-post, side by side, but not close. **Scully** *moves towards her, inch by inch. There is a pause*]

Scully: Er . . . what do you wanna do, Marie? When you leave school. Well, I mean, I know y' never there, but –

Marie: Our Karen said she'd try and get me in her place. If I want.

Scully: [*Nearer and nearer*] What does she do, your Karen?

Marie: She's in the meat processin' factory on the industrial estate. She takes the guts out of chickens. She's

the fastest in the factory. [**Scully** *stops moving towards her.
There is another pause*] But what I really wanna do is leave
this place.

Scully: What for?

Marie: [*She glances at him, and speaks flatly*] You've seen
the toilet walls. You heard that lot on the bus tonight.

Scully: Ah, I wouldn't worry Marie.

Marie: You don't have to.

Scully: Mmmm well ... [*As his almost last resort,* **Scully**
drags Tony's cigarettes out of his pocket, and looks at
Marie, *staring ahead. He gets out a box of matches and two
cigarettes. He lights them like lovers always do on the
pictures, gets nearer to* **Marie**, *and slips her a cigarette*]

Marie: No thanks – didn't you know? I've just given up.

[**Scully** *looks at his two cigarettes, then looks at* **Marie**. *He
starts to smoke two cigarettes as if it is the normal thing to do.*
Marie, *when he isn't looking, smiles to herself*]

Scully: Funny enough, I'd more or less stopped as well ...
With ...

[*A boy comes past on a bike, glances in, goes on, stops and
looks back at* **Scully's** *two cigarettes.* **Scully** *puts one
behind his back quickly, and glares at the lad, who goes
on*]

Marie: Footballers shouldn't smoke.

Scully: I know, that's why I ... [*Throwing the cigarettes
away*] I had stopped really, I just thought ... [*He shudders,
and bangs his feet on the ground*] Brrr, gone a bit cold
though, hasn't it ... All of a sudden like.

[*He puts his hands in his pockets, and fidgets with his undies.
He stops. He edges his arm around her shoulder.* **Marie**
looks down demurely – and sees his shoes. She begins to

giggle. **Scully** *half laughs with her, but then stops as her giggles turn to laughter. She doubles up*]

Scully: Oh – hey! What's the matter now!

[**Scully** *looks down, and sees where he has had his feet. Two small pools of talcum powder have congregated around his shoes.* **Scully** *leans back against the wall of the shelter and puts his hands in his pockets. He closes his eyes.*

   Marie *takes pity, and puts her arm around his shoulder*]

Scully: [*Opening his eyes*] It was – I sort of spilt – it was . . . it's talc . . . the lid . . . came off. [*He motions*]

Marie: I really like you, y' know, Francis . . . you make me laugh.

Scully: Oh great. Go out with Jimmy Tarbuck then.

[*She puts her other hand inside his jacket and around his waist, and blows in his ear. He tries to stare resolutely ahead, but not for very long. He looks at her*]

Scully: Is that all I do – make you laugh?

Marie: Oh no. You have no idea . . . You're really soft underneath it all, aren't you? [*Blowing all the time*]

Scully: If those're compliments, I don't want to hear the insults.

Marie: I bet you're really gentle and generous and kind . . .

Scully: Leave off, Marie – y'll have to stop readin' 'True Romances'. Wake up, will y' – I'm not a doctor, an' you're not a nurse an' I haven't just performed major surgery on y' dad – or y' dog. [*She looks at him*] . . . Er y' can keep blowin' in me ear though, if y' want . . .

[*She does so. No one has ever blown in his ear before*]

Marie: An' strong as well. Really, really . . . strong.

Scully: Well, y' gettin' closer now . . .

[*He turns towards her. He puts his arm around her shoulders and kisses her – a long kiss. We hear dirty cheap laughter – a grown-up's sniggering.* **Scully** *and* **Marie** *look up.*

We see **Isaiah** *framed in the entrance to the shelter, wildly beside himself as* **Marie** *and* **Scully** *break apart. We see a police car behind* **Isaiah,** *with* **Mooey** *peering out of the back*]

Isaiah: Well well, they said you'd be here – the tea-leaf and the bike, like a fairy story. With an unhappy ending. For you, Scully.

Scully: Take no notice, Marie, it's only another courtin' couple.

[**Isaiah** *moves forward, hurls* **Scully** *away from* **Marie** *and out of the shelter.* **Scully** *is bounced onto the path outside and against the railings on the promenade*]

Scully: What was that for?

Isaiah: Because I've wanted to do it for a long time, and now I've got a good reason. Get in the car. You're under arrest, plums.

Scully: What y' arrestin' me for?

[*He looks around. There is a second police car behind* **Isaiah.** *Its boot lid is up, but we cannot see why.* **Scully** *is pushed hard towards the first police car, and bounces off the side of it*]

Isaiah: I'm arrestin' you for burglary, Scully. Burglary. [*He laughs*]

Scully: Y' makin' it up as y' go along.

Isaiah: I suppose I'm makin' up a portable television set, a painting, three flyin' ducks and the contents of a fridge?

Scully: I never did *that*!

Isaiah: Is that a fact? Well then, tell me, how come your little friends have confessed, and your fingerprints are all over the house? [*He laughs joyously*] Hey? Hey? [*He continues laughing as he bundles **Scully** into the back of the car and almost into **Mooey's** lap. **Isaiah** climbs into the car, completely overwhelmed*]

Scully: What about her?

Isaiah: [*Glancing out*] She can walk herself home. You were warned, Scully. I told you not to mess around with me. Nobody messes with me . . . [*The car moves forward*]

Mooey: [*In a theatrical whisper*] The others made me go back, Scull – I er, didn't want to – all I got was a tin of spam . . . I wanted the ducks but they wouldn't let me have them . . . er, this is er it's er . . . I don't like this kind of excitement.

[**Isaiah** *laughs some more – he can't control himself. He turns and looks at **Scully** in total bliss and laughter. **Scully** looks away*]

Scully: Jeez, the laughin' policeman . . .

[*We fade as we see the two cars moving away amid manic laughter. We see **Mad Dog** and **Snotty Dog** in the back of the second car. Then we see the pram sticking out of the back of the boot. We just hear a baby beginning to cry as they move away and **Marie** comes out of the shelter and walks slowly away*]

Episode 7

Scully's dream of being a professional footballer

Episode 7

1 **A waiting room at the police station**

We see **Scully, Mooey, Mad Dog** *and* **Snotty Dog** *in a police waiting room.* **Mad Dog** *and* **Snotty Dog** *sit together.* **Mooey** *is apart from them.* **Scully** *is apart from the others. He is generally not at his most attractive in the earlier part of the scene.*

Scully: [*After a long pause*] What are y', hey? What are y'?

[*A pause*]

Mad Dog: It was your big idea in the first place.

Scully: Yeah, to take the balls, nothin' else. Did Isaiah mention anythin' about balls, hey did he?

Mooey: He er, said somethin' about them to me, he also said he'd er, brin' tears to me eyes.

Scully: I told y', didn't I – I told y' in the house – she would never have had the nerve to report us f' that, but the minute y'robbed the slightest thing that was theirs, y'may as well have took the whole house brick by brick.

Mad Dog: It was her, laughin' at me dad on the zebra crossin' like that. I wanted to kill her . . . y' know, like . . . really really kill her.

Scully: Since when has anyone ever been killed by a portable telly, three flyin' ducks an' a paintin'?

Mooey: An' er, a tin of spam. Er y' could've poisoned her spam, Mad Dog.

Mad Dog: [*Really angry*] Shut up, Mooey! You snitched on us anyway.

Mooey: No I never.

Snotty Dog: They picked you up first – you must have told them.

Mooey: But er they knew more about it than I did.

Scully: I'm not surprised, if the rubbish you were comin' out with in the toilets is anythin' to go by, Mad Dog. Probably half the estate knew before the Leighs themselves found out. An' if you think that's doin' somethin' big . . .

Mad Dog: [*Genuinely*] I never told anyone about the robbin', I swear I didn't . . . [*After a slight pause*] I wanted to but . . .

Scully: Yeah, an' while we're at it, Mad Dog, thanks for the escort to Otterspool Prom. Much appreciated. You'll find out how much later.

Mad Dog: It was only . . . a joke, an' if you hadn't have made a fool out of me in the toilets I –

Scully: [*With spite*] It's you who're the joke, the pair of y' – I laughed for a while, but the joke's wore thin now. Anyway, if y' really want t' know, I only knocked around with y' 'cos y' made me look good.

Mad Dog: [*With more spite*] Didn't work then, did it?

Scully: [*Laughing harshly*] Mad Dog, you could make a motorway accident look good.

[**Scully** *looks away to see* **Isaiah** *standing in the doorway. He enters and closes the door behind him. He flourishes their statements*]

Isaiah: Now now, ladies . . . I'm happy to announce that the forensic evidence combined with your touching little statements of guilt –

Scully: I never robbed nothin'.

Isaiah: Be quiet, scum-bag – put together means that you are well and truly 'nicked', as they say – and you will duly appear in court, and then, with a little bit of luck, depending on if I can arrange who the magistrate is, you'll get put away. Well, *you* will anyway, Scully. Ah, happy days ... We're tryin' to find your parents, but there's a lot of pubs on this estate. Which reminds me – we've found your father, Scully, he's downstairs now, drunk and disorderly.

Scully: All right, all right, big deal – so what happens now?

Isaiah: Oh ... a nice long wait, unfortunately without refreshments of any kind, nor place to rest your weary head, while we scour the town for your parents. Eventually. But we're far too busy at the moment to spare anyone. Should be a bit quieter about five this mornin' though. We'll try then.

Scully: Me mam'll be in the Labour Club.

Isaiah: She won't be at five this mornin'.

Scully: I wanna see her now.

Isaiah: Y' could always try an' escape. [*He smiles invitingly, and moves away from the door*]

Scully: Y' know, f' every policeman like you, Isaiah ...

Isaiah: [*Savagely*] Don't call me that!

Scully: Y' know, f' every policeman like you, I bet there's probably another fifty who wander around doin' no harm to no one, just doin' their job – y' know – keepin' the peace. An' none of them stand a chance because of dick-heads like you.

[**Isaiah** *advances.* **Mad Dog** *and* **Snotty Dog** *look at each* *other.* **Mooey** *puts one hand between his legs and another over his eyes.* **Isaiah** *goes down on his haunches in front of* **Scully**, *and leers up at him. Suddenly he puts his hand up.* **Scully** *inevitably flinches away and ducks.* **Isaiah** *puts his hand on* **Scully's** *shoulder*]

Isaiah: Now that would have made me very angry once. Very angry indeed. Because that wasn't nice. What I would have expected from a foul-mouthed little no-mark like you, Scully. But still, not very nice. However, it doesn't matter now, does it? Not now. Why should I get angry now? . . . Oh incidentally, why don't you confess to the rest while you're here? Might help you – in the long run.

Scully: The rest of what?

Isaiah: Oh, the seventeen other burglaries that bear all the hallmarks of last night's little effort.

Scully: Go an' play with y' truncheon, will y'?

Isaiah: Amazing similarities really. The same time of night, the same entries, the same sort of things stolen. The –

Mooey: Er includin' a tin of spam?

Isaiah: I'm sure it was you lot, certain.

Scully: Get lost.

Isaiah: [*Turning to* **Mad Dog** *and* **Snotty Dog**] How about you, boys, want to confess now?

Mad Dog: It wasn't us – you know it wasn't us.

Isaiah: But let's just say . . . let's put it this way, if you two were to confess to all the other robberies, and you were to implicate –

Mad Dog: Wha'?

Isaiah: Implicate . . . it means 'to frame' really – but if you were to implicate your friend and mine, sweet little Francis here, now I might just find it in my powers to blow in a few people's ears, tell them how much you were led astray by someone or other . . . what good boys you are really . . . I'm sure that the powers that be would take a *very* lenient view. Boys . . . [*A pause*] After all, there didn't seem too much love lost from what I could hear before.

[**Isaiah** *sits down between* **Mad Dog** *and* **Snotty Dog**, *affably. There is a silence.* **Mad Dog** *and* **Snotty Dog** *look at* **Scully**, *who looks at them, bleakly but without threat.* **Isaiah** *looks at all of them*]

Mad Dog: But we didn't do them.

Isaiah: It wouldn't matter. You'd get a suspended sentence, a small fine, in smaller payments, soon forgotten.

Mad Dog: [*Head down*] And he'd get done for . . .?

Isaiah: Seventeen burglaries.

Mad Dog: I've never done anything like this before, but . . .

Isaiah: Yes, go on . . .

Mad Dog: [*Fidgeting*] And I don't really know how to say it.

Isaiah: It's simple really – just say it.

Mad Dog: [*Slight pause; then with an icy savageness*] Fair enough. Piss off Isaiah!

[**Isaiah** *is about to hit* **Mad Dog** *over the top of his head with a clenched fist but there is a knock on the door.* **Isaiah** *leaps away from the* **Dogs**, *and leans against the table in the middle of the room. He speaks gently and sweetly*]

Isaiah: Enter.

[*A* **Policewoman**, *holding the Dogs' baby brother, opens the door, somewhat harassed*]

Policewoman: Sergeant, there's a ... [*She glances at the boys*] ... there's a couple of women at the desk – you'd better see them now.

[*We hear* **Mrs Scully'***s voice roaring down the corridor*]

Mrs Scully: Y'll do more than see me, y' bent bastard!

Isaiah: [*Leaving the room*] It's funny how characteristics run in the family isn't it?

[*He closes the door. The lads are left alone.* **Scully** *and* **Mad Dog** *look at each other. Finally,* **Scully** *nods his head in some acknowledgement.* **Mad Dog** *shrugs. There is another pause.* **Scully** *doesn't look at him as he speaks*]

Scully: Y've just done something big, Mad Dog.

[*We see* **Mad Dog** *almost refuse to accept the compliment, then grow into it. Finally he grins at* **Snotty Dog** *and sits up straight. We see* **Snotty Dog** *do the same. Soon it will be his compliment* . . .]

2   The front desk at the police station

Mrs Scully *is signing a surety for* **Scully***. In the background, we see* **Mrs O'Gorman** *knocking* **Mad Dog** *and* **Snotty Dog** *almost through the plate glass window of the police station entrance.* **Snotty Dog** *is pushing the pram, and the pram bounces back off the door.*

   Mooey *is peeping out of the waiting room.*

Mad Dog: [*Faintly from outside*] Y' never complained last night, Mam, when y' were watchin' the midnight movie in bed. [*As she smacks him*] Ooow!

Isaiah: [*Politely*] What are you going to do to raise the surety, Mrs Scully – sell the portable television?

Mrs Scully: Say that when there's witnesses about, Scarface.

Isaiah: [*Very clenched*] I wouldn't dream of doing such a thing, madam.

Mrs Scully: Course you wouldn't. [*To herself as she turns*] Have a nice time, Mooey.

Isaiah: Rest assured, Mrs Scully, we will provide him with the finest service available. I will personally see to it myself. [*He turns away as* **Scully** *and* **Mrs Scully** *depart. He sees* **Mooey** *sadly watching in the corridor*] Get in there, pea-brain, an' stay there!

3   The steps of the police station

We see **Scully** *and* **Mrs Scully** *walking down the steps outside the police station, and* **Marie** *walking towards them, looking tired and carrying her high-heeled shoes.*

Mrs Scully: [*To* **Marie**] Unless y' can afford fifty pounds, Marie, don't bother.

Marie: I haven't even got fifty pence – I've had to walk all the way from Otterspool. [*She looks slyly at* **Scully**] I knew where you were though – I followed a trail of talcum powder.

[**Mrs Scully** *looks at them both in some puzzlement.* **Scully** *looks away*]

Scully: Sorry, y' know, about . . . leavin' y' like that.

Marie: As I remember it, you didn't have much option. [*She keeps walking on to the station, and looks over her shoulder*] . . . Have a good trial, Francis . . . the football kind, that is . . .

[**Scully** *and his mother walk towards the roadway*]

Scully: Where are y' going to get the money from?

Mrs Scully: Never you mind.

Scully: But fifty pounds! Where would you get it from?

Mrs Scully: Never you mind.

Scully: But I do.

Mrs Scully: Well, don't . . . Did you rob anything?

Scully: Nah. Not a sausage. Or a tin of spam. But I did break in.

Mrs Scully: I've had it then.

Scully: I know.

Mrs Scully: Stupid.

Scully: Absolutely, Mam. Completely. Utterly. Totally. Stupid . . . The trouble was I thought it was foolproof, but the others proved me wrong . . .

Mrs Scully: Better get your head down, when you get in. Big day tomorrow . . .

[**Scully** *grimaces. She casually links his arm. They walk down the road together, and approaching them are* **Tony** *and* **Rita** *Rita is crying but threatening, and ahead of* **Tony**]

Tony: No, y' see, Rita . . . I know it's going to be difficult for us . . . for you . . . but – hallo Mam! [*He stops*] Er, see y' then Rita . . . y'll understand one day Rita . . . [*We fade as* **Tony** *joins them*] Er, listen Mam, er when y've got a minute, there's somethin' you'd better know . . . it's er good news really, Mam . . .

4 Scully's home

We see **Scully** *arriving home.* **Mrs Scully** *and* **Tony** *go into the back kitchen.* **Scully** *goes briefly into the living room, sees*

Mrs Barrett *looking cataclysmic, and leaves immediately.*

Next, we see **Scully** *about to get into bed, looking at his wrecked pair of football boots. He is naked apart from his undies. With his back turned, he flicks at the front of his undies, and a cloud of talc still emerges. He turns and does a flying header onto his bed.*

5   Dream Sequence

We see **Scully** *in a dinner jacket at a reception with* **Dickie Davies** *and* **Isaiah** *either side of him. They are at the 'Footballer of the Year' reception, at the top table, underneath the banner 'Young Footballer of the Year'. The trophy is in front of* **Scully** *and he is making a speech which appears to be confident, articulate and amusing. He turns and indicates* **Kenny Dalglish***, who has also received an award.* **Dalglish** *moves into frame, past* **Dickie Davies***, and holds up his trophy for 'Footballer of the Year'.* **Dalglish** *puts his arm around* **Scully***, and together they hold up their trophies.* **Scully** *raises his other arm, and we see that he is handcuffed to* **Isaiah***.* **Scully's** *face drops as we see* **Isaiah's** *hand go up too.*

6   Scully's bedroom

We see **Scully** *wake up. He has an alarm clock raised above his head as he lies in bed, his arm around a pillow, and a silly grin on his face. He looks to the next bed to see if* **Arthur** *has seen him. He sees* **Dalglish** *looking at him from* **Arthur's** *bed, and drops the alarm on his head. He turns back to* **Dalglish** *in the next bed. We now see* **Arthur,** *with a couple of curlers in his hair, looking at him.*

7   The classroom

We see **Scully** *in class, desk lid up, looking out of the window. He is lost in day-dreams, as he watches the kids playing games on the school fields. We hear noises of 'Franny Scully' as if sung by the kop choir drift in and out. A pair of well-polished football boots come flying into his desk, waking him up. He looks up.* **Bignall** *has dropped them in. He gives* **Scully** *a quiet wink as he goes away.*

8   The school dining room

We see **Scully** *in close-up in the dining room. He is miles away yet again, a knife and fork in his hands, staring out. We see the others on the table looking at him. He makes cutting motions with his knife and fork. The camera moves back to reveal that he is cutting up tapioca to little effect – especially when he tries to eat it.*

9   The school hall

We see **Scully** *in the wings at the pantomime rehearsals, with his head against the side of the proscenium arch, looking at the clock at the back of the hall. It indicates three-thirty. We see* **Joanna** *giving him the cue for his entrance . . . once . . . twice . . . three times.* **Mrs Heath** *climbs on stage, goes across to him, and touches him gently on the shoulder. He jumps and looks up.*

10   The school corridor

We see **Scully** *and* **Steve** *walking down the corridor towards the school exit. The clock indicates five past four.* **Dracula** *and* **Castanets** *await them at the door, like doormen at the*

Adelphi Hotel in the centre of Liverpool. **Scully** *carries the kit he needs in a plastic bag.*

Scully: Y' heard about last night.

Steve: The trouble? [**Scully** *nods*] Yes, I heard.

Scully: And?

Steve: As you should know, in this country, a man should be presumed innocent till proven guilty.

Scully: But I am guilty ... sort of.

Steve: Yes, I noticed. I've never seen so many games of football in the school yard ...

11   Outside the school

Dracula *swings into stride with them as they walk towards the car park.* **Castanets** *tries to, but trips himself up with his broom.*

Dracula: Good afternoon, sir. The pantomime going well, is it, sir? The highlight of the year, that's what it is. Everyone concerned should be congratulated. [*He looks at* **Scully** *as* **Castanets** *catches up*] It's things like that what make a school tick.

Castanets: Tock ... Tick.

[**Steve** *stares straight ahead and keeps walking.* **Dracula** *and* **Castanets** *flank* **Scully** *and* **Steve**. **Castanets** *is having difficulties*]

Dracula: And it's good to see lads like young Francis, with all their problems, using up their energies, extending their range.

Castanets: Rover. [*Twitches*] Range ... Range Rover? Come here, hey. Come here Rover.

[*He whistles at an imaginary dog*]

Dracula: [*Desperately trying to say the right thing*] One thing for sure, Mr Stevens, Francis here, all the confidence in the world – that's what he's got. We've all had our ups and downs, and Francis has had several, but come the first night, have no fear, this boy here, he won't be nervous.

Castanets: Breakdown ... Wally ... [*Stops*] Wally, I think I'm crackin' up ... down, you shake it all – Wally, I'm serious. I keep repeatin' things, things, 'Things like a walk in the park, things like ...'

Dracula: And all the very best tonight, son. [*He waves his broom*] Anytime you want to use the gymnasium in the future, I'm your man, I'll always be here.

Castanets: 'There and everywhere ...'

[*As he breaks into the Beatles song, **Dracula** moves back towards him while **Scully** and **Steve** walk on with quiet contempt. When **Dracula** reaches **Castanets** the song is brought to an abrupt and painful end. **Steve** opens his car door, and **Joanna** goes past **Scully's** side as he waits to get in*]

Joanna: [*Flatly, without looking*] Good luck.

Scully: [*Quickly going after her*] Joanna ... [*He stops her*] Look, you know y' said you were too busy, with the panto, to like ... and I'm busy now as well –

Joanna: In more ways than one.

Scully: Yeah, but y' know when it's over, if ... would you fancy going out with me? Then? Hey?

Joanna: I don't think so – I always make it a rule not to come between courting couples.

[*She walks off. **Scully** is about to protest about 'courting couples' when **Steve** peeps his horn. **Scully** walks back to* *the car.* **Dracula** *is walking back into school, defeated now by* **Castanets'** *full-blooded version of 'We'll Meet Again' as he waves to* **Steve's** *car*]

12 Inside Steve's car

We see **Scully** *in* **Steve's** *car, driving towards Liverpool's training ground, expressionless but tense. He finally speaks.*

Scully: Will any of the others know each other at this trial?

Steve: One or two will, but they won't know many . . . Your team, the trialists, will probably play Liverpool's Youth team. [*He turns to* **Scully**] They'll know each other. So it'll be a hard game. But don't worry – it'll be hard for all the others as well.

13 The training ground car park

As they talk we see them sweep into Melwood, the training ground, and on to the car park. **Steve** *stops the car at the far end of the car park, near the dressing rooms.* **Scully** *gets out of the car, with his head down. He looks up, and walking towards him, no more than five yards away, in training gear, is* **Kenny Dalglish**, *with one of the Liverpool training staff.* **Scully** *says what every lad would say.*

Scully: All right, Kenny!

Dalglish: [*With barely a glance*] All right son.

[**Dalglish** *jogs towards the pitches.* **Scully** *goes to walk after him as if to touch him.* **Steve** *whistles at him.* **Scully** *stops and goes back towards the dressing rooms, still looking over his shoulder at* **Dalglish.** *Other trialists are gathering on the steps*]

14   The dressing room

We see **Scully** *in a crowded dressing room as he gets changed with the other trialists. A* **coach** *hands out an old away strip for the lads to wear, calling out their names as he goes.* **Scully** *is sitting down, head down, staring at the floor.*

Coach: Oakley, Pye, Dayus, Barnes, Hope, Hannaway, Haigh, Linnett, Long, Scully, Roberts ... play the positions you normally play boys.

[**Scully** *sits up on the call of his name, puts his hand up, and gets a shirt – it is thrown at him. He looks around. Quite a few lads seem to know at least one other person there. Just a couple are as alone as* **Scully.** *The* **coach** *quietens them, and stands at the doorway*]

Coach: All right lads, listen now, a few words of advice – remember how we play here at Liverpool – it's a team game, not an opportunity for fancy pants and posers to show off – no one's going to be at all impressed by nutmegs and tricks – just do the simple things today. [*He looks around*] Out you go. And enjoy yourselves!

[*There is some rueful laughter as the lads troop out*]

15   The pitch

We see the trialists coming out. From the opposite dressing room we see the opposition – a year or so older, quite deliberately, and dressed in Liverpool's red strip, laughing and joking and mugging about. There is a professional contempt very quietly knocking about.

As they approach the pitch, we see **Dalglish** *jogging up and down nearby, doing turns and short sprints.* **Scully** *inevitably watches him as he walks. He goes past one or two of the opposition who are also watching* **Dalglish.**

Scully: What's he doing here?

Player: [*Curtly*] Fitness test. Doubtful for Saturday. [*They jog away*]

[**Scully** *looks away, and sees* **Steve** *on the touchline. He nods towards him*]

16   The pitch

[*Author's note: In this sequence, all the other players should be of a high county standard – apprentice, professionals or amateurs with Liverpool F.C., and* **Scully** *must be,* at the very least, *of such a standard to be very secure of his place in any school team.*]

We see the kick-off. **Scully** *is playing inside-left, one of the attackers in a four–three–three formation with* **Scully** *often going wide on to the wing. The game is cruel.* **Scully** *gradually sinks out of his depth. His commitment is manifest for most of the game, but his contribution is slight to the extreme. Time and time again he is caught in possession, hits poor passes or loses battles for space and pace. They aren't giving him anything.*

At half-time we see him head down, from a distance, already slightly away from the rest of the team – or they are slightly away from him. He stands with his hands on his knees, head down. The only time he looks up he sees **Dalglish** *walking back towards the dressing room behind* **Steve**. *He focuses on* **Steve**. *Neither of them have any expression.*

The game goes on – and on. **Scully** *begins to give up. He is well down and beaten, near to tears, as the final minutes approach. Nobody is passing to him, and nobody bothering to mark him – he catches sight of* **Dalglish** *as he leaves the dressing rooms in casual clothes and walks along the touchline towards his car.* **Dalglish** *stops a few yards away from* **Steve**, *and begins to watch the match casually.*

Scully gives it one more go, and every time he is near to **Dalglish** *the ball is taken away from him, or he gives it away. At first* **Dalglish** *is unaware, then begins to realize that possibly, for a change, a fan is on the pitch and he is on the touchline. Then, as* **Scully's** *attitude becomes more and more intense, as the game enters its very final stages, he finds* **Scully** *looking more at him than the match, to the point that* **Scully** *is facing the wrong way when a ball comes towards him from a misplaced opposition clearance. There are groans and some ridicule and snarls. The ball rolls towards* **Dalglish** *for a throw-in.* **Scully** *goes towards* **Dalglish.** **Dalglish** *hits the ball towards him.* **Scully walks past the ball towards Dalglish. Dalglish** *looks around.* **Scully** *stands facing him.*

Scully: Speak to me. Speak to me. Come on – tell me you're there. This time you're there – the first time I don't want you to be – and there you are!

Dalglish: What?

[Some of the players and some of the staff approach, as does **Steve***]*

Scully: I'm useless, tell me, it's all right, just tell me, I'm flippin' useless.

Dalglish: Look son –

Scully: It's all been a dream. Nothin' but a soddin' dream. Why were you there in the first place? You bastard! You bastard!

[He begins to prod **Dalglish,** *and pushes him hard.* **Dalglish** *grabs hold of his arm, not to hurt but to stop him.* **Scully** *is pulled away by* **Steve** *and some of the staff and players. They push him away as if he had a disease, till* **Scully** *is knocked over, away from the pitch and distanced from* **Dalglish.** *He lies there with only* **Steve** *close to him, the others looking at him with contempt.*

A whistle blows and the game continues. **Dalglish** *moves away, towards his car, occasionally looking back.* **Steve** *picks up* **Scully,** *and moves him towards the dressing rooms.* **Dalglish** *turns his car around, and backs up near* **Scully** *and* **Steve**]

Dalglish: [*Winding his window down*] Is the boy OK?

Scully: I was going to be just like you. [**Steve** *indicates to* **Dalglish** *that it's all right, and takes* **Scully** *away*] You knew didn't y', Steve, you knew all along I was no good.

Steve: Not 'no good'. Don't think that. Just . . .

Scully: Yeah, yeah, leave out the missin' words, I can fill them in meself.

17 The dressing room

We see **Scully,** *almost dressed, his back turned, as the others sweep sweaty and bubbling into the room. He silences them without any effort, or intention.*

He turns around and goes out of the room as soon as he can, not looking at anyone.

18 Steve's car

We see **Steve** *in his car, the engine ticking over, waiting.* **Scully** *approaches, opens the car door and sits down. The car goes. As they leave the ground,* **Scully** *looks around, as if looking for the last time. He turns back and faces the front.*

19 Scully's road

We see **Scully** *getting out of the car at the school. It is going dark.* **Scully** *leans into the car to* **Steve.**

Scully: Next time y' wanna destroy some dreams, Steve, pick on someone else.

Steve: I thought I was doing the right thing. I was trying to ... It was meant to help.

Scully: [*Flatly*] Join the Samaritans. [**Scully** *walks away towards his house*]

Steve: [*Calling after him*] But you know what you're good at, Scull!

[**Scully** *slouches towards a corner. Around the corner come* **Mad Dog**, **Snotty Dog** *and* **Mooey**.

They are armed with rucksacks, fish and chips, a bottle of Tizer, and in **Mooey's** *case, all his wordly possessions in one plastic bag plus a plastic seaside yellow bucket.*

They are already trying to hitch-hike. **Mooey** *thumbs a milk float, with the hand that he is holding his chips with. Very quietly, unseen by* **Mooey,** *his chips fall from their paper to the floor.*

Scully *doesn't really want to see them.*

Snotty Dog *is holding a map of Great Britain and looking at it as if it was a* Playboy *centrefold, holding it at all angles*]

Mad Dog: [*With slightly false enthusiasm*] All right Scull! We were just lookin' for you. Are y' comin' or wha'?

Scully: No thanks. [*He goes to go past*]

Snotty Dog: It's the Shetlands, Scull! We're goin' the Shetlands!

Scully: [*Not believing them*] Y' wha'?

Snotty Dog: Diggin' f' oil!

[**Mooey** *cheerfully holds his bucket up*]

Mad Dog: [*Out of the corner of his mouth, looking around*] We're doin' a Ronald Biggs, lah! [*He nods*]

Scully: He went t' Brazil, not the north of Scotland.

Snotty Dog: Oh, so that's ...! [*He looks again at the map*]

Mad Dog: But it's a start, Scull.

Scully: An' a finish.

Snotty Dog: [*Almost to himself*] I told y' it wasn't Southern Ireland ...

Mad Dog: But if we *can* get a start an' make some fast money, we can go anywhere we want, with no one to stop us.

Snotty Dog: An' no one need know who we are.

Mad Dog: Or what we've done. [*In a hushed tone*] We can all adopt new identikits.

Scully: [*Bluntly*] Y' cracked. Y' must be. Y'll never make it, an' even if y' do, there'll be nothin' down for y'.

Mad Dog: [*Madly*] But anythin'll be better than being stuck around here waitin' to get put away.

Scully: [*With the slightest hesitancy*] Y'll be missed in no time.

Mad Dog: No we won't, I've got it planned. It's Saturday tomorrow, right? The Law won't even know we've gone till Monday when we're supposed to report. They might not even bother lookin' for us till Tuesday. That's at least three whole days. See: brains. [*He points to his head victoriously*]

Scully: I don't know ... nah.

Mad Dog: Chicken.

Mooey: An' donkeys. There's donkeys up there an' all, Scull.

Scully: Ponies. An' anyway, I haven't got any money.

Snotty Dog: We've got some.

Mooey: I haven't. [*He looks down*] Who stole my chips?

Mad Dog: We'll lend you some, pay us back when y' get y' first week's wages on the oil. Y' won't miss it out of two hundred and fifty quid! [**Scully** *laughs, and walks away*] All right, all right, y' don't have t' come, we've got a map . . . [*After him as he goes*] Just think, we all used t' look up t' you once . . .

[**Scully** *smiles, grimly*]

20   Outside Scully's house

We see **Scully** *approaching his house. A* **young girl** *walks towards him, pushing a pram and one screaming baby. We overhear her words to* **Scully.**

Young girl: Y' haven't seen Snotty Dog O'Gorman have you . . .?

[**Scully** *virtually ignores her, and goes down his own pathway.*
   The front door bursts open and **Mrs Barrett** *comes racing out, holding her eye. She briefly tries for dignity, then scatters towards her own house*]

21   Scully's hall and living room

We see **Scully** *entering the hallway of his house. He looks back, but not for long.*
   We hear **Rita's** *fury like a woman scorned as she faces and bangs against the downstairs toilet door. We hear, too, a loud recording of late trains at Lime Street Station, coming from the living room.*

Rita: You're dead, Tony Scully, d' y' hear me, y' dead after this!

Tony: [*From behind the toilet door*] Don't talk to me like that, you bitch – I'm a man!

[**Rita** *becomes hysterical – a mixture of laughter and tears.*

Scully *looks at her briefly, and then turns towards the living room.*

He sees **Arthur** *looking pretty, moving well, and balancing a book on his head to achieve a more attractive walk.*

Henry *has his headphones on, attached to the music centre. He is mouthing words of his recording, sitting in an easy chair, with a British Rail cap strapped to his head.*

The television is on – a fashion show perhaps.

Arthur *saunters up and down.*

Scully *stares around him, and listens.*

He snaps **Henry's** *headphones off his head and looks down at* **Henry**. *There is quiet desperation in his voice . . .*]

Scully: Speak to me, Henry . . . anything. Anything . . . normal. Sane . . . reasonable. [*Raising his voice*] *Speak to me!*

[*There is a pause.* **Henry** *expresses surprise, panic, hesitancy and then considerable thought. He finally speaks*]

Henry: One of our trains is missing.

[*He nods, points his finger knowingly at* **Scully**, *and then grins, madly.*

Scully *lets* **Henry** *take his headphones back, and walks out of the room into the hallway.*

he grabs a raincoat off the bottom of the bannisters.

He walks out of the house, to the noise of tears, trains, television and **Arthur** *breaking into sudden song – 'I feel pretty, oh so pretty'*]

22 The M6 – Haydock intersection

We see **Mad Dog**, **Snotty Dog** *and* **Mooey**, *at the motorway approach road.*

It is raining.

Mad Dog *and* **Snotty Dog** *smile their warmest, thumbs out, to each car or lorry. When the vehicle doesn't stop, the thumb turns into two fingers.*

Meanwhile, slightly behind them and ignored, **Mooey** *has reversed the process. He is giving two fingers at approaching cars, and then thumbing them as they go.*

As we move away from them, we see that they are hitching by the side of the 'Birmingham and the South' approach road sign.

We also see **Scully** *approach them, and move them towards the 'Scotland and the North' slip road.*

23 The M6

It is raining even more. The joy has left **Mad Dog** *and* **Snotty Dog.**

Mooey *upturns his bucket, and water pours out.*

A couple of lorries and cars go by. Then a lorry pulls up, brakes steaming, and turns down the slip road.

They go racing, the **Dogs** *barging to the front, and all four try to pile in.*

Scottish driver: Eh, hang on, lads, where y' goin'?

Mad Dog: Y'know, the Shetlands, where the oil is.

Scottish driver: Arr, I'm no much good t'yer then, Glasgow's as far as I'm goin', an' no further.

Snotty Dog: That's all right, mister, we'll go an' see Celtic play.

Scottish driver: But, sonny, the Shetlands're a long way away from Glasgow.

Snotty Dog: Are they?

Mad Dog: [*To* **Snotty Dog**] Yeah, of course they are, don't you know nothin'? But it doesn't matter, pal, there's no panic, we'll start work on Monday, come 'head.

[**Mad Dog** *and* **Snotty Dog** *pile in, but* **Scully** *stays where he is.* **Mooey** *tries to climb on board as well*]

Scottish driver: Only the two of y', son, that's all I can take.

[**Mad Dog** *tries hard not to look pleased, while quickly closing the door*]

Mad Dog: Oh well, er, Scull, y'll soon catch us up on the road.

Snotty Dog: Yeah!

Mad Dog: We'll wait for yer in Glasgow, all right?

Scully: [*Smiling*] Deffo, boys. See y' there, at the match.

Mooey: Last one stinks. [*The lorry blows diesel smoke all over them as it goes and, as it goes,* **Scully** *two-fingers them with both hands, expressionless.* **Mooey** *looks at him, the lorry and then back to* **Scully**] Er, what y' doin' that for, Scull?

Scully: Nothin' Moo. Just a message f' the Dogs, that's all.

Mooey: Oh er yeah. [*He does it vigorously as well.* **Scully** *has already stopped.* **Mooey** *stops*] Er aren't we friends with them no more?

Scully: Y' could say that, lah.

Mooey: What happened? Did we have a fight?

Scully: Not so that y'd notice.

Mooey: An' er y' sure y' not friends with them no more?

Scully: We haven't been friends f'a long time, Mooey.

Mooey: I know.

Scully: So, why are y' askin'?

Mooey: I er, just want t' make sure.

Scully: Make sure of what?

Mooey: That y' not friends with them no more.

Scully: Oh hey, Moo!

Mooey: So that y' won't hit me when I tell y' what they said about y' behind y' back.

Scully: Oh aye?

Mooey: Er yeah, they didn't want y' to' come with us t' see them donkeys, y' know, they would have gone without y', but –

Scully: They didn't know how t' get there without me.

Mooey: Well, er, I think so.

Scully: Any more bits of gossip, while y' at it?

Mooey: Er no. [*He looks down at his feet, and then back at* **Scully**]

Scully: Come on, y' may as well tell me, I won't get upset.

Mooey: Y' certain y' not friends with them?

Scully: I won't be friends with you in a minute!

Mooey: Well er, there was the paint, Scull.

Scully: What paint?

Mooey: The er, paint they used t' write all those dirty things about you an' our Marie on the walls –

[**Scully** *grabs hold of* **Mooey**. **Mooey** *tries to curl up – on his feet*]

Scully: Who told you? Come on, who told yer? *How d' y' know*?

Mooey: 'Cos er, I helped them, Scull.

[**Scully** *throws* **Mooey** *away from himself.* **Mooey** *covers himself up in case* **Scully** *kicks him. Nothing happens, except that* **Mooey** *gets muddy.* **Scully** *stares into the distance.* **Mooey** *gets up and looks into the distance too*]

Scully: Wait till I see them!

Mooey: We'll see them tomorrow.

Scully: Will we?

Mooey: Er, don't get me muddled, Scull, I thought we were meetin' them in Celtic, like, y' know, y' won't tell them it was me, will y'?

Scully: How much money y' got on y'?

Mooey: I haven't got any money on me, Scull.

Scully: There y' are then, neither have I.

Mooey: But ... but they said y' didn't have t' pay for y' donkey rides up there. They said it's free an' y' can get cheap pullovers an' all.

[*Although they haven't been thumbing lifts, a car pulls up past them. The driver beeps his horn.* **Mooey** *goes to race off*]

Mooey: Yis!

[**Scully** *grabs him by the lower arm and stops him*]

Scully: No.

[**Scully** *takes the plastic bag off* **Mooey**, *opens it and lifts out a pair of undies, a pair of football shorts and shirt, and a battered treasured teddy bear.* **Mooey** *shrugs and takes the teddy bear back.* **Scully** *half sighs, half smiles, and turns* **Mooey** *around. He puts the rest of the stuff back in the bag, and puts the bag over* **Mooey's** *wrist.*

They start walking away. **Mooey** *once wistfully turns*

back towards the car as it moves off. They start walking towards the westbound carriageway of the East Lancs road]

Mooey: They made me do it, y' know.

Scully: It's all right –

Mooey: I didn't want to, I told them I couldn't spell, but they said –

Scully: Forget it.

Mooey: I told them you were my best friend and –

Scully: [*Gently*] Yeah yeah, just get a move on, will y'.

Mooey: Er, like, where we goin'?

Scully: Home.

Mooey: I er, thought y' wanted t' see the Dogs?

Scully: Knowin' them, I'll see them soon enough.

Mooey: But er . . . wha' about the donkey islands?

Scully: Y' don't really want to' go there, Mooey.

Mooey: Don't I?

Scully: No.

Mooey: Oh, OK. But why're we goin' home?

Scully: We're goin' home to face the music, Moo.

Mooey: Array, do we have to? I hate dancin'.

[*We fade as they walk along together*]

24   Scully's house

Scully *opens the door leading from the hall to the back kitchen, and walks into the back kitchen. He sees smoke coming from the grill on the cooker, and* **Tony,** *in a haze, sitting at the table, head in hands, and back turned.*

Scully: Tony . . . Tony! The toast is on fire! [**Scully** *goes across through the smoke to switch the grill off*]

Tony: Oh aye, yeah.

Scully: And that's the last of the bread.

Tony: Is it?

Scully: Yeah – I don't know whether to throw it in the bin, or say a prayer over it.

Tony: [*To himself*] Oh, God in Heaven.

Scully: You can say the prayer if y' want, I don't mind. [*He looks at the cooker*] The cooker's on.

Tony: I know.

[**Scully** *opens it. A steak pie suffering from first degree burns lies there, and smoke belches out of the cooker.* **Scully** *slams the cooker door shut and turns the gas off*]

Tony: That was the last pie as well. [*He gets a packet of cigarettes out, and fumbles with them*]

Scully: [*Despairingly*] What's the matter with you, Tony!

Tony: Who, me?

[*He can't get the cellophane off the cigarettes.* **Scully** *looks in the larder, and settles for a tin of beans. He throws them in a pan, and lights the gas.* **Tony** *still can't get the cellophane off. His hands are shaking. He throws the packet on the table*]

Tony: I'm getting married.

Scully: [*Stunned*] Y' wha?

Tony: You heard.

Scully: Bloody hell . . . when?

Tony: A week on Saturday.

Scully: Have y' dropped one? [**Tony** *finally nods his head*] Does Rita's mam an' dad know about it?

Tony: No.

Scully: It'll finish Rita's career, y' know. No one'll fight a pregnant wrestler. [**Tony** *shakes his head*] Does me mam know?

Tony: I told her last night.

Scully: Y'll have t'tell Rita's mam and dad soon.

Tony: No I won't – I've just told Rita – she can tell them. [*He starts to struggle, successfully this time, with the cellophane on the packet*]

Scully: [*The penny half drops*] Y' mean she doesn't know she's pregnant?

Tony: Rita isn't pregnant, Francis. I'm not marryin' her.

Scully: Well, who are y'marryin' then?

Tony: Mrs Barrett . . . I'm marryin' Mrs Barrett. [**Tony** *gets a cigarette out and lights the filter tip*]

Scully: Ah go 'way with y', y' havin' me on.

Tony: I'm not.

Scully: Y've lit the wrong end.

Tony: I don't care. [*He tries to smoke it*]

Scully: She's old enough to be y' mam.

Tony: I know.

Scully: Y' can't be.

Tony: I am.

Scully: How long has this been goin' on?

Tony: Months. It all started the night she told me I was irresistible . . . I've always had this attraction to older women.

Scully: But Mrs Barrett . . .

Tony: Yeah well – she's worth a few bob, y' know. Her last husband left her a lot.

Scully: That won't happen with you anyway. All you'd leave her is y' Giro and a bag full of washin'.

Tony: I still can't believe it.

Scully: I know. Neither can I.

[*There is a pause.* **Tony** *finally glances up*]

Tony: Y' beans're burnin'.

Scully: I know.

[*They both sit there*]

25   The living room

We see **Scully** *and* **Tony** *watching the television.* **Gran** *comes in through the front door, cackling fit to bust, enters the living room, and comes between* **Tony** *and the television.*

Gran: You an' Florrie! [*She laughs uproariously*] You an' Florrie! I heard it at bingo. It's the talk of the town! No one could concentrate on their numbers. [*She laughs again*] Where y' goin' to live?

Tony: With her.

Gran: Where though?

Tony: Next door. Get out of the way, Gran, it's 'Bugs Bunny'.

Gran: [*Going towards the back kitchen as* **Mrs Scully** *comes in through the front door*] Next door, next door – that's the best yet! Did y' hear that, Bernadette – our Tony leaves home at last! Where does he go? Next door!

[**Mrs Scully** *stands in the door. She looks at* **Scully** *as he goes past*]

Scully: Don't ask, Mam. Just don't. [*He goes out. She lets him go*]

26 Scully's bedroom

We see **Scully** *in his room. He is taking down his pictures of Dalglish. Not angrily. He drops them on the floor of the room by the door. Also, in the background, we see* **Arthur's** *pictures of women by his bed.*

Scully *hears the front door slam shut, and goes to look out of the window. As he does so,* **Arthur** *comes into the bedroom, wearing his mother's dressing gown.* **Arthur** *looks at the pictures of Dalglish, at* **Scully** *at the window, and at his own pictures of skin care and make-up application. He begins to take off his mother's dressing gown.*

We return to **Scully,** *looking out of the window. We see* **Mrs Scully** *and* **Gran** *linking arms with each other, and* **Tony** *being joined at the gate by a shy* **Mrs Barrett***. He walks with her. After a bit she links on to his arm. He tries to fight it at first, but gives in. The* **two elderly gents** *at the gate then follow at a discreet distance.* **Scully** *half smiles at the sight, then turns. He sees* **Arthur***, wearing a pair of football shorts, taking down his lipstick pictures. He has moved the Dalglish pictures to his bed. He glances around at* **Scully.**

Arthur: I'm sick of bein' a girl. Girls have babies. Even when they're old an' ugly ... [*He puts up a picture of Dalglish*] And if you're a girl, you can't play football for Liverpool ... [*He looks at Dalglish*] that's right, isn't it, Kenny?

[**Scully** *glances at us, then closes his eyes. He looks back at* **Arthur,** *and goes towards the door*]

Scully: Sweet dreams, Arthur ...

27 The living room

We see **Scully** *asleep on the couch. The adverts before 'News at Ten' are on television. The living-room door opens, and we see*

Mrs Scully. *She looks at* **Scully**, *asleep, hesitates, and then wakes him up.*

Mrs Scully: Francis, Francis –

Scully: Sod off, Dalglish! . . . Wha'? [*'News at Ten' starts, and* **Scully** *looks around*] Has the party finished at the Labour Club?

Mrs Scully: No, it'll be a while yet. It must be costin' Florrie a bomb – all the drinks are on her.

Scully: So what're you doin' back this early?

Mrs Scully: I'm goin' to make some sandwiches for after . . . and I didn't feel much like drinkin' tonight. What with you an' Tony . . . and one or two other things. [*She goes to go out of the door*] Why don't you go down to Wong's and get yourself some chips?

Scully: Y'll have to give us some money then, I'm broke.

Mrs Scully: There's a pound in me pocket. Take that.

[*She goes towards the back kitchen.* **Scully** *goes towards her coat hanging on the bannisters. There is a knock on the front door.* **Scully** *answers it. We see* **Mooey** *who is looking very happy.* **Mrs Scully** *is looking out from the back kitchen door. She approaches finally*]

Mooey: Oh aye, er, excuse me, Mrs Scully, there was a feller in your side alley, er I've just seen him, honest, deffo, really. Er.

Mrs Scully: There couldn't have been – I've only just come in a minute ago, and I never saw anyone. Are y' sure it wasn't the shadows?

Mooey: Er, it might have been, but er, when I asked if there was anyone there, the er, shadow ran right through Mrs Barrett's entrance an' into her back garden.

Mrs Scully: Well, if there was someone, he'll be well gone now.

Mooey: Er yeah ... [*Cunning comes over his face*] But er, I bet that I've er, saved you from bein' burgled, you know, er.

Scully: Do you have to mention burglary?

Mooey: Er yeah, otherwise no one gives me a reward. [*He looks hopeful*]

Mrs Scully: [*Laughing*] Give him fifty pence Francis, an' now clear off from under my feet, the pair of you, and let me make these sandwiches for when they come back.

Mooey: [*As* **Scully** *gives him fifty pence*] Yis! Are y' havin' a party? Can I come?

Mrs Scully: *No*! Go on, go an' get some chips. And take your time comin' back, Francis. I want half an hour on me own ...

28 Outside Scully's house

Scully *looks back at her as he goes. He walks along with* **Mooey** *to their gate.* **Mooey** *grins at him, casually jangles his pockets, and winks.*

Scully: Y' almost had me believing you.

Mooey: Good hey ... but er there *was* someone in your alley, Scull.

[**Scully** *stops and looks back. They are at the corner of the road*]

Scully: See y' after, Moo. [*He turns away.* **Mooey** *goes to follow him*] I said I'll see you later. [**Mooey** *nods, but still follows*] Here, take my money. If I'm not back, get y' self a special. [*He gives him the pound note.* **Mooey** *turns and walks away immediately*]

Mooey: Yis! Double Yis! ... An' er, yis again ...

29   Scully's garden

We see **Scully** *as he climbs over fences and sneaks towards his own back garden. He gets to the next door garden opposite to* **Mrs Barretts'**s *and waits in the shadows by the coal shed, watching his own back kitchen. A dog howls, but otherwise it is silent. Then we see and hear* **Mrs Scully** *unbolt the back door to the kitchen. She gives a couple of loud coughs. Finally, quietly . . .*

Mrs Scully: Are you there . . .?

[From behind **Mrs Barrett's** *coal bunker, we see a man emerge, go out of* **Mrs Barrett's** *entry door, and then through the Scullys' entry door, slipping inside the house. He has his coat collar up and his hat down. He is barely seen before* **Mrs Scully** *closes and bolts the back kitchen door.*

We see **Scully** *edging towards his house. He climbs over the next door neighbours' coal bunker into his own back yard and creeps towards the back kitchen window. He sees that the curtains aren't quite shut, kneels below the window and then comes slowly up.*

We see **Mrs Scully** *and the man with their backs turned. He has his arm around her, and his head over her shoulder as she butters some bread. We can hear her talking but only the mumble of words. Then, as* **Scully** *watches, we hear his mother laugh warmly, like a young girl. She puts the knife down and turns sideways – so does the man. He puts his arm around her, and we see it is* **Dracula,** *grinning . . . We see* **Scully** *in shock, but still looking]*

30   'Dracula' sequence

We now see what **Scully** *is 'seeing' – an insert like a scene out of a genuinely horrific movie:* **Dracula,** *in fangs and gown and* *blood, leers above* **Mrs Scully** *and her white uncovered neck. He throws his fangs into her neck, and blood spurts everywhere. She tries to push him away in terror, and staggers against the back kitchen table, knocking things over. Then she falls against the cooker, to be bitten viciously again. Blood is flying in torrents as* **Mrs Scully** *scatters again, trying to protect herself.* **Dracula** *drags her down onto the floor and aims for her neck again, so much in love.*

31   Scully's garden

We see **Scully**, *his head against the window, hardly able to look. We now see the reality of what he is looking at. We see* **Dracula** *in normal dress gently kiss the side of* **Mrs Scully's** *neck, then her cheek. They put their arms around each other. They kiss each other, and hold the kiss.*

Scully *drops from view at the window. We see him outside, on his knees, by the grid for the overflow from the sink. He is trying to retch. He stops and begins to stand up.*

From his point of view we see **Mrs Scully** *playfully pull away from* **Dracula**, *take the knife off the table and point it at him. Then she grins and drops the knife back on the table.* **Dracula** *puts his hand on her dress at the shoulder, pulls the strap down and flicks at her bra strap. Again she picks the knife up and points it at him. He takes the knife off her and throws it on the table. They embrace and kiss again.*

He slowly begins to unbutton the back of her dress. We see **Scully** *biting on his hand. He falls to the floor. He goes on his hands and knees and retches into the grid. He then stands up, looking as evil as 'Dracula' ever was, and storms towards the back entry door.*

32   The back entry to Scully's house

We see him running down the entry, to the front of the house.

Almost before he has turned out of the entry, he is banging at the front door, knocking on the knocker, and also using his fist.

Scully: Come on out, Dracula! Come on, I know you're in there, come on, y' fang faced bastard, come out! [*He bangs and bangs*] You touch me mam, you just touch her!

[*We see a movement of curtains at the front window.* **Scully** *bangs on the window as well, then back to the door. Finally* **Mrs Scully** *opens the door. Curtains on the block are being lifted*]

Mrs Scully: [*Almost as angry as him*] For God's sake, Francis, what's got into you – what's the matter?

Scully: Dracula's in there an' he's . . .

Mrs Scully: He's what?

Scully: He's . . . he's with you.

Mrs Scully: So? Is that reason to wake the dead?

Scully: But I seen him. I seen him hidin' in the garden.

Mrs Scully: Rubbish. He came in the front way after you'd gone. He was only returnin' my purse. I'd left it in the club.

Scully: Don't lie to me Mam, not you. Don't!

Dracula: [*Coming out of the front room, smirking*] Y' mother's not lyin', young Francis. She left her purse on the table in the club. Then it sounded as though there were keys in there, so I followed after just in case she couldn't get in the house.

Mrs Scully: And then I invited him in for a cup of tea.

Dracula: That's right.

Scully: He doesn't drink tea, and y' a liar, y' both liars – if I hadn't have come back, he'd have got his fangs right in, same as he did with Mrs Barrett and now he's –

Mrs Scully: Francis, shut up, right now. [*She makes a grab for him, but misses*]

Scully: I won't shut up and y' haven't seen nothin' unless he goes.

Dracula: [*Showing his true colours*] You – you be careful what you say – I'm up to here with you. [*He points to his forehead*]

Mrs Scully: Francis, I'm warnin' you, I'll give you the hidin' of your life when I get you inside.

Scully: I'll say what I want, Dracula, and you won't get me inside the house, Mam, not after he's been there. [*He moves away*] You should have left me in the police station, I'd rather be battered by Isaiah than find out about you two.

Dracula: [*Grabbing for and getting hold of* **Scully** *and throwing him against the wall of the house*] Yeah, go ahead, you run away, you jump bail, it'll be all right, you won't suffer, y' never do. It'll be me who'll pay, if you jump bail.

[**Scully** *looks at him*]

Dracula: Fifty quid I'll fork out if you frig off, an' d' y' know what, it'll be worth it if this is all the thanks I get, y' little snot. Where else d' y' think y' mother gets the money these days? The trees? Y' stupid brothers? Y' grandmother? Y' drunken father?

[**Scully** *spits in his face and* **Dracula** *lets go of him.* **Scully** *throws a wild swing at* **Dracula***, and hits him on the side of the head, knocking him, this time, against the wall.* **Mrs Scully** *tries to grab* **Scully.** *He runs to the front gate, in tears*]

Scully: Y' gettin' y' money's worth tonight though – aren't y'? Well worth fifty pounds. D' y' have to pay for all y' women, Dracula? Is that the only way y' can get them?

[**Dracula** *runs at him, and* **Scully** *runs too. So does* **Mrs Scully**. **Scully** *runs the fastest, and away.* **Dracula** *stops, and* **Mrs Scully** *reaches him.* **Scully** *turns around. His mother shouts*]

Mrs Scully: It's not true – it's not true!

Scully: But it is!

[*We focus on* **Scully** *as he runs, tears streaming down his face. He runs right into* **Mrs Barrett** *and* **Tony**, *walking home, followed by* **Gran** *being supported by the* **two elderly gents**, *singing 'My Blue Heaven'*]

Tony: What's wrong with you?

Scully: It's me mam – me mam – she's had Dracula in.

Tony: I know – they left the club together. So?

Scully: So he was with her – he was with me mam.

Tony: So what? Live and let live, I say, hey Florrie?

Mrs Barrett: She'll have a good time with Mr Moss, generous to a fault he was.

Scully: Oh shut up, stupid!

Tony: Hey hey, now then, that's no way to talk to my fiancée.

[**Scully** *puts his hands to his eyes*]

Gran: Y' mother's entitled to some pleasure. I don't know how she sticks it with you lot sometimes. Y' need a few gin an' tonics to go home to that house. I know I do. Good luck to them, I say. [*Laughing*] Maybe we'll have another weddin'.

Scully: Y' just as bad as him – y' all are – y' don't care about nothin' – least of all y' selves – y' just stewin' – that's all – well, I'm not an' I never will. I'm goin' an' I'm never comin' back!

[*There is laughter from all of them.* **Scully** *turns and runs away. As we follow him, we listen to* **Tony** *and co.*]

Tony: Tara then – go on, Florrie, tell me again, y' know, the bit about lookin' like Burt Reynolds' younger brother . . .

Gran: Hey, I've just had a thought, Florrie – as soon as they've stopped y' child allowance, y'll be entitled to a pension! [*She roars with laughter again*]

Mrs Barrett: I don't think that's very funny . . .

Tony: Go on though – me an' Burt . . .

33   A road

We see **Scully** *running as if forever, through his estate, across the main road, past the pub and the youth club and his school, and towards the middle-class estate – and* **Steve's** *house. We see him get there, and knock on the door, in the dark. We hear footsteps on the stairs again, and see a woman in a dressing-gown. She puts the safety chain on the door before she opens it.*

Scully: Is Steve there, please?

Mrs Steve: No I'm afraid he's not. He's at a meeting.

Scully: Will he be long?

Mrs Steve: I have absolutely no idea. Is it important?

Scully: Yes.

Mrs Steve: Can I take a message?

[*She is a rather formal, cold lady, deliberately distancing herself from the tear-stained, crumpled figure on her doorstep. A* **girl's** *voice is heard from upstairs*]

Girl: Mummy, who's there?

Mrs Steve: Nobody darling, go back to sleep.

Scully: [*Bitterly*] Yeah, nobody.

Mrs Steve: Pardon?

[*He shakes his head*]

Mrs Steve: Can I take a message?

Scully: No. Forget it!

Mrs Steve: Are you sure?

Scully: Certain.

Mrs Steve: Who shall I say called?

Scully: [*Walking away*] Kenny Dalglish. Tell him Kenny Dalglish.

Mrs Steve: [*Softening*] Are you quite all right?

Scully: I'm great. Never felt better. In fact, I'm going out to paint the town red ... [*He walks away. It turns into a run*]

34   Outside the school

We see **Scully** *in close-up, painting. We move away to see that he is painting on the largest exterior wall in school. He is painting in scarlet-coloured, twelve-foot letters, the legend 'Dracula Sucks'.*

35   Inside a police car

We see **Isaiah** *and a* **police driver,** *parked up at the dim side of a row of shops. They are eating a takeaway meal – chips, pie, peas and gravy – like pigs. A message comes over the radio to them.*

Voice: Foxtrot four one, come in, foxtrot four one.

Isaiah: Yeah all right, but I'm not going anywhere till I've finished me pie.

Voice: Getting reports of graffiti –

Isaiah: I hate Italian food. [*He laughs, and has to nudge his companion*] 'I hate Italian food'!

Voice: – reported all through the estate. Someone paintin' 'Dracula' bloody everywhere. Including the back of the police station, the town hall steps, the windows of the 'Bow and Arrow', the forehead of a tramp in Jubilee Park, and the deep end of the outdoor swimming pool.

[**Isaiah** *and the* **driver** *look at each other*]

Isaiah: Can you repeat the last one?

Voice: The outdoor swimming pool. It's been drained since we found the piranha fish in there, remember?

Isaiah: All right, we'll keep an eye open. [*He switches off, crushes the remains of the takeaway, wipes the paper around his mouth, and goes to get out of the car*] The back of the police station! [*He gets out*] Huh, how could they get away with that? What do they do in there on nights, hey? [*He throws his tray and paper in a bin and turns and goes to walk back to the police car. As he looks at it, his legs almost buckle in shock*]

36   Outside the sports shop

We see **Scully** *standing in front of the sports shop window, facing the huge life-size picture of* **Kenny Dalglish.** *At the side of the picture is a dummy with Liverpool's kit on –* **Scully** *is slump-shouldered, red-handed and carrying the paint tin – a large one.*

Scully: Not a word. Y' finished now all right. Well, that suits me.

[**Scully** *goes to walk away. He hears* **Dalglish's** *voice. He whirls around and sees* **Dalglish** *where the dummy was, modelling the kit*]

Dalglish: O I don't know, I've quite enjoyed myself.

[*As* **Scully** *turns and raises the paint tin to hurl it, we see* **Isaiah's** *police car, suitably inscribed with a big red Dracula on its side, slide to a halt behind* **Scully.**

We see **Isaiah** *grin with relish as he realizes who it is. We see* **Scully** *hurl the paint tin straight through the window.*

We freeze frame as the window smashes, the picture of **Dalglish** *gets soaked in red paint, and the dummy is knocked to the ground*]

Follow-up Activities

Episode 1

1 Kelly says of Mooey that he's only 'a loony from the silly school'. Mooey replies, 'Er, no, I'm not. I'm just a bit slow.'

   Bleasdale has said of Mooey that he is either one of the great geniuses of our time or totally mad. 'He never knowingly loses, and is the only person in the whole series who is truly happy.'

   What is your opinion of Mooey? What is there to like or even envy about him?

   Should people whose abilities are limited in some way be the object of humour in television programmes?

2 *On probation* When a person is found guilty of committing a crime, he or she is given a sentence. The sentence may be a punishment (i.e. it is designed to make the guilty person suffer in proportion to the wrong or harm he or she has done) or it may be a deterrent (i.e. it is intended to discourage the person from doing the same thing again). Or it may be a sentence intended to reform the guilty person.

   Often a court places a young offender 'on probation' in the hope that he or she will be reformed under the supervision of a probation officer. The probation officer supervises the person for a period of between one and three years.

How useful and helpful is Scully's probation officer? Will he be successful in reforming Scully? Why (or why not)?

3 Almost certainly, Scully's probation officer will have to write a report on each of his meetings with Scully. Write a short report (of less than 200 words) in which he records his aims in having this interview with Scully and in which he describes briefly and factually what happened.

4 Do you think Scully brings trouble on himself or do people 'get on his back' unfairly?

5 In what ways are daydreams important? How can they be dangerous?

6 'Actin' is only for the birds.' What does this statement tell us about Scully?

7 Write a short story about a girl or boy who is always day-dreaming.

8 Describe a time you have tried to get out of doing something at school which a teacher wanted you to do but which you dreaded doing.

Episode 2

1 Do you care about the appearance of the area in which you live? Do trees improve an environment? In what other ways can a city environment be improved? Do you agree with Scully when he says, 'They wanna plant some factories then'? Why does the woman say, 'Communists!'?

2 Alan Bleasdale based scene three of this episode on the following passage from his novel, *Scully*:

When we got to the Park there was this big crowd over by the bowling green; all these old dodgers in their best clobber, and blokes taking photos and everything. Even the St John's Ambulance were there. We went over and had a look. Mooey and a few other nutters were already there. They was the only ones under sixty.

'What's goin' on?' I said.

'They're buryin' trees,' Mooey said, 'diggin' holes an' buryin' them.'

'Oh, I'm sorry,' I said, 'I didn't know it was a funeral.'

'Oh no,' he said, 'they're not dead. They're only buryin' them.'

'Well, they soon will be dead,' Mad Dog said. 'Fancy plantin' trees at this time of year. They must be daft.'

'Hey,' I said, 'hark at David Bellamy here.'

I went and had a closer look. There was a bloke stood on a little platform making a speech. Behind him was this sign on a board. It said, 'PLANT A TREE YEAR'. He had a chain around his neck, this feller, and the misery-hole sitting next to him in a fur coat, she had one on too. I couldn't hear what he was saying proper 'cos he was speaking to his chain and the first two rows. After a bit he went over to the trees, dug a little hole, stuck a tree in it, said a quick 'Hail Mary' or something, and then did a quick sprint with his missus over to this big car with a badge painted on it, and every one went home.

There was about a dozen of them. Nice little trees too, as trees go. All labelled and everything. All these posh names in some foreign language.

'Mooey,' I said, 'Are y'doin' anythin' tonight?'

'No,' he said. 'Shall I bring me spade?'

What changes has he made? Why do you think he made each of them?

Choose another short scene from this episode and re-write it in story form.

3 Choose a short scene from a novel. Try adapting it as a television script.

4 What do you think are the causes of vandalism? Think of an area you know that suffers from vandalism.

What could be done to decrease or prevent the problem?

5 Imagine breakfast time in the Scully household. In story form, write a description of that scene.

6 *The police*   The police may stop you and search you if they have 'reasonable suspicion' that you are carrying stolen property (or drugs or firearms). They can arrest you if you are found committing, or attempting to commit, any offence which carries a penalty of five years in prison for a first offence (which includes theft).

Is Isaiah within his rights in the scene at the end of this episode? Do you think he does or says anything wrong?

How do you think the police can best prevent crime? Should this be their main function?

7 Make a list of the points that you think make a good police officer. Compare your list with others in your group.

Episode 3

1 Debate the advantages and disadvantages of staying on at school after reaching the school-leaving age.

2 Improvise the scene that might take place between Mrs Heath, Kelly and Brian Bignall after the end of this episode.

3 Improvise Leslie Brady's next meeting with the head teacher.

4 Discuss who you think is to blame for the maths lesson getting out of control. What would you have done if (as a new teacher) you had been giving that class that lesson?

5 Suppose Steve or Mrs Heath were to give Brady's replacement some advice about taking Scully's class. In list form, write down the tips they might give.

6. Write a description of 'The Ideal Teacher'.

7 Suppose in one family there is a sixth former with a Saturday job, an unemployed eighteen-year-old and a twenty-year-old who has a job but who is saving up to get married. Improvise (or write about) a discussion in which they talk about how much money they give to, or get from, their parents each week.

8 Suppose Joanna keeps a diary. Write what she might say about Franny Scully (up to the end of episode three).

Episode 4

1 What makes a good youth club?
2 Write a story or poem about a time when you have been out with nothing to do and nowhere to go.
3 'There was a time when a cottage by a ford, growing into a village by a bridge, a city on a great trading river, could be the forerunner of a community ... Today we lack time. New estates are made to grow in a few months.'

    What are the problems of living on a new estate?
4 'When a block of high-rise flats is built, what we have really done is to turn a street on end' – *a planner.*

    What does a tower block of flats lack that a street has? Investigate the problems of living in a block of flats for (a) young mothers, (b) teenagers and (c) old people. What can people who have to live in such buildings do to improve their lives?
5 'I can see y' future planned out right there ... petty crimes, a little mugging, a few burglaries, Borstal, gaol ...' How accurate do you think Isaiah's prediction of Scully's future will prove to be?
6 Write a story about an event which could have been disastrous but which you are able to laugh about now.

Episode 5

1 How well does Scully get on with girls? What do you think is (a) Joanna's and (b) Marie's honest opinion of him?
2 Do you think the *Scully* plays reinforce a sexist view of women?
3 Are women and men shown to be equally powerful (or weak) in the plays?

4 Write a story called 'When parents split up'. In your story, you might concentrate on what the children say and do. They may feel anger, sadness, surprise, fear, guilt, embarrassment or even relief.

   Write a second episode to your story in which one parent makes a new friend. How do the children react then?

5 Is Mrs 'Crackers' right to keep the footballs?

6 If someone broke into your house, would you expect the police to take action?

7 Why does Mrs Scully say, 'No dreams are soft. Keep y' dreams as long as y' can, son'? Is it good advice?

   What does Scully mean when he says, 'Other people have got their dreams for me as well – even softer than mine'? What are the problems (and advantages) of other people having dreams for you?

Episode 6

1 Why is Steve concerned about Scully?

2 Marie says, 'What I really want to do is leave this place.' Debate the advantages and drawbacks in 'moving away'.

3 She also says to Scully, 'You're really soft underneath it all.' Do you agree? How 'hard' is Scully?

4 How will Joanna feel when she hears about the events of this episode?

5 Plan, improvise, rehearse and present your own modern pantomime. It could be based on a traditional story but take place in well-known local setting. It might also comment on local issues.

Episode 7

1 Does Scully like Mad Dog?

2 Scully respects him for 'doing something big' (page 182). Do you think he has done something admirable?

3 Do you think Isaiah is really corrupt? Does Scully think he is a 'typical' policeman?

4 Is it cruel or 'kind' of Steve to organize a Liverpool trial for Scully? (How did Steve expect Scully to do in the trial?) 'I thought I was doing the right thing,' he says (page 194). Was he?

5 Write a story about the Dogs and their attempt to run away from home.

6 Suppose Tony writes a letter to a magazine's 'Problem Page'. Write the letter that he might send and the answer that might be published with his letter.

7 'Sweet dreams, Arthur,' says Scully. What makes him say this?

8 In the Mrs Scully–Dracula episode, who do you think is in the right and who is in the wrong? How does Mrs Scully feel towards Franny at this point?

9 For which characters, if any, is there a happy ending?

10 What do you think will happen to the main characters in the future?

General

1 What career advice would you give Scully? Would he take it?

2 In the *Love and Marriage* volume in this series, there is a play called *Gulpin*. It is about a girl who is a fan of Liverpool F.C. Is it 'odd' that a girl should be interested in football? What do girls think of football and football fans?

3 Do you think boys have a better time than girls in inner city areas and on new estates?

4 Who is *your* hero? Why?

5 In your wildest dreams, what would you like to be doing when you are twenty-five?